English World

Student's Book

8 B1

MACMILLAN

Mary Bowen, Liz Hocking & Wendy Wren

Unit	Reading	Reading comprehension	Looking at language	Grammar
1 A website project Page 7	*The www project* a leaflet giving advice and guidance	literal questions; expressions; thinking skills; vocabulary; personal response	nouns *-tion / -sion* noun + noun	revision of main tenses: present simple and continuous; past simple and continuous *I speak French. Today I am learning Italia* *Last year I went to Spain.* *I was travelling for ten hours.*
2 We ♥ New York Page 17	*New York! New York!* Study skills: proofreading; personal account	literal questions; expressions; spotting mistakes; thinking skills; vocabulary; personal response	adjectives *oy / oi* conjunction *because*	order of adjectives *She wore an unusual, old, Chinese, silk shawl.*
3 Different places Page 27	*The White Giraffe* a story from another culture	true/false questions; meanings of phrases; thinking skills; definitions; personal views	verbs *gh sounding /f/; silent gh* conjunctions; sentences with three main clauses; suffix *-ness*	past perfect and past perfect continuou *He had seen a strange bird.* *It had been flying above the trees.*
4 A great destination Page 37	*Bangkok – The Grand Palace* a guidebook	literal questions; subjects of paragraphs; thinking skills; definitions; personal views	adverbs *-ture / -sure* complex sentences	reported speech: statements and commands *John said that he was tired.* *The teacher told the boys to sit down.*
5 Beyond this world Page 47	*Hello, Earth* science fiction	true/false questions; meanings of phrases; adverbs; thinking skills; definitions; personal views	compound words *y sounding /ɪ/ or /aɪ/;* informal styles in fiction; prefix *trans-*	reported speech: statements, past to pa perfect, present perfect to past perfect *Lucy said that she had never been abroa* *The old man said that had grown up in India.*
6 I remember Page 57	*The honey-seller* autobiography	literal questions; meanings of phrases; thinking skills; parts of speech; personal views	derived words silent *t* subordinate clauses	time clauses: all tenses with *when, after while, before, until, as soon as* *When the bell rang, they went in.* *As soon as our guests had gone, we went to bed.*
7 Questions, questions Page 67	*A desert map* detective fiction	literal questions; meanings of phrases; thinking skills; definitions; word classes; personal views	words with two or more meanings *-ous* direct speech in fiction	pronouns: subject, object, indirect object possessive; possessive adjectives *They saw us.* *I gave the flowers to her.* *The book is mine.*
8 In my view Page 77	*Text messaging – GR8 or not?* different opinions	literal questions; expressions; adjective definitions; thinking skills; vocabulary; personal response	words with two or more meanings (2) *-ise / -ize / -yse* pronouns	reported questions; *if / whether* *The teacher asked if anyone was absent.* *We wondered what the strange sound was*
9 What a wonder! Page 87	*And the winners are …* a magazine article	multiple choice questions; defining phrases; thinking skills; vocabulary; personal response	words with two or more meanings (3) *-ary /-ery / -ory* clause order; prefix, *over-*	passives: present and past continuous *The house is being designed by a famous architect.* *A play was being performed in the park.*
10 Communications Page 97	*The First Nations* letters, emails and texts	literal questions; thinking skills; multiple choice questions; definitions; personal views	phrases *au / aw* conjunction *so*	third conditional *If he had passed his exams, he would have gone to university.*
11 I'm going to talk about … Page 107	*Giving a class presentation* Study skills: advice about giving a presentation	literal questions; expressions; vocabulary; thinking skills; personal response	phrasal verbs silent *u* compound adverbs suffix *-dom*	future continuous *This time next week we will be enjoying ou holiday.*
12 A new website Page 117	*Global Youth Link* a website	literal questions; meanings of phrases; thinking skills; definitions; personal views	synonyms tricky words tones in writing; suffixes: *-age, -ship*	*either / or, neither / nor* *You can choose either burgers or pizza.* *Neither Sally nor John passed the exam.* past perfect passive *The house had been damaged by a violent storm.*

Grammar extra Pages 127–130   Projects Pages 131–135

Grammar in use	Class writing Independent writing (WB)	Listening and speaking
future: *will* and *going to* *The lesson will finish at ten o'clock.* *He is going to become a doctor.* present perfect simple/continuous *She has never been abroad.* *I have been waiting for half an hour.*	Features of writing to advise SB: advice for taking a trip abroad WB: advice for a friend expecting a visitor from abroad	**Conversation practice:** the *www project* topics **Listening comprehension:** the assignment of the topics **Individual speaking (WB):** the project topic I would choose
see, hear, watch, feel something *happen/ happening* *I saw the boy fall.* *I watched the snow falling.*	Study skills: proofreading, correcting and re-writing texts SB: proofreading/correcting a text WB: proofreading/rewriting two texts	**Conversation practice:** photos of NY **Listening comprehension:** a presentation about the Statue of Liberty **Individual speaking (WB):** talking about two local sights of interest
expressing purpose: *so (that), (in order) to* *She went to the library so that she could study in peace.* *He went to the sports centre to have a swim.*	Features of stories from other cultures SB: a story about travel in own country WB: a story set in own school	**Conversation practice:** photos of Australia **Listening comprehension:** an interview about the Great Barrier Reef **Individual speaking (WB):** talking about a place of outstanding beauty or importance
present simple for fixed future events *Our train leaves in ten minutes.*	Features of writing to inform / persuade SB: a guide to the Grand Canyon WB: a guide to a local place	**Conversation practice:** schools **Listening comprehension:** a discussion about two very different schools **Individual speaking (WB):** talking about your school
quantifiers: *(a) few, fewer, the fewest, (a) little, less, the least* *Our team scored the fewest goals.* *There is little water left in the lake.* *Joe shows the least interest.*	Features of science fiction writing SB: a boy's first visit to the Moon WB: continuation of the story	**Conversation practice:** performance arts **Listening comprehension:** a tour of the Globe Theatre **Individual speaking (WB):** talking about a theatre or cinema visit
agreement: *so do I, so will you, so must he, neither / nor do I* *"I love the holidays." "So do I."* *"I can't swim." "Neither can I."*	Features of autobiographical writing SB: an autobiographical event from notes WB: a true autobiographical incident	**Conversation practice:** schoolwork and hobbies **Listening comprehension:** Laura and her parents talking about her schoolwork and the website project **Individual speaking (WB):** talking about time for schoolwork and hobbies
reflexive pronouns *She looked at herself in the mirror.* *The children made the cake themselves.*	Features of detective writing SB: an investigative interview – Luke / Miranda WB: an investigative interview – Miranda and the bookshop owner	**Conversation practice:** environmental disasters **Listening comprehension:** a TV programme about an oil spill disaster **Individual speaking (WB):** researching and recounting an environmental disaster
exclamations: *what, what a / an, so, such a / an, such* *What clever girls!* *It's such a big car!* result clauses: *so / such a / such … that* *The film was so bad that we left.*	Features of writing about opinions SB: different opinions about a subject WB: different opinions about a subject	**Conversation practice:** losing things **Listening comprehension:** monologues about items people have lost **Individual speaking (WB):** talking about an event when something important was lost
adjective + preposition: *good at, keen on, interested in, etc* *John is good at sport.* *New York is famous for its skyscrapers*	Features of magazine articles SB: a magazine article from notes WB: researching and writing a magazine article	**Conversation practice:** eating habits and preferences **Listening comprehension:** a questionnaire about healthy eating **Individual speaking (WB):** talking about your daily diet and how healthy it is
wish + *would*, past, past perfect *I wish he would stop shouting.* *Sally wishes she had a pet.* *Fred wishes he had worked harder.*	Features of formal and informal letters SB: a formal letter of enquiry WB: an informal letter to a friend	**Conversation practice:** environmental problems **Listening comprehension:** the project leaders talking about environmental issues **Individual speaking (WB):** talking about local environmental concerns
question tags *You like animals, don't you?* *They haven't arrived yet, have they?* *We mustn't be late, must we?*	Study skills: preparing for a class presentation SB: notes for a class presentation WB: preparing a class presentation	**Conversation practice:** using computers **Listening comprehension:** Laura's presentation about the project **Individual speaking (WB):** talking about creating a student website for your school
adverbs of degree + adjective (+ adverb) *It's rather cold today.* *That man is incredibly rich.* *She sings really well.*	Features of evaluative writing SB: evaluation of the Global Youth Link website WB: evaluation of a real website	**Conversation practice:** the website **Listening comprehension:** team leaders talking about the website **Individual speaking (WB):** giving your opinion of the website

Ross, Holly, Laura and her brother Jack are from Hampton in the UK. A few months ago, they entered a competition entitled "A portrait of our town" – and they won! Their prize was a wonderful trip to New York.

Ross, Laura, Holly and Jack did not know that young people in other countries all over the world had also entered the competition. When they arrived in New York, they met the winning teams from eight other countries. They spent a fantastic week in New York and made lots of new friends.

Professor Brown
Professor Brown, the organiser of the *Portrait* project, was also with them in New York. On the last day of their trip he had a surprise for them. All the teams were going to work together on a new project. It was going to be very exciting!

Dr Naseer   Georgi Dolidze
They also met the international co-ordinator, Dr Naseer, from Egypt, and Georgi Dolidze, a young website designer from Georgia, who had helped to judge the *Portrait* project.

Carrie, leader of team from Brisbane, Australia

Usha, leader of team from Jaipur, India

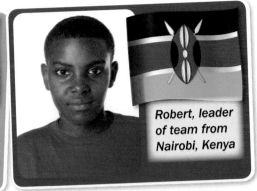

Robert, leader of team from Nairobi, Kenya

Brad, leader of team from Vancouver, Canada

Tippi, leader of team from Bangkok, Thailand

Ali, leader of team from Amman, Jordan

Sofia, leader of team from Manaus, Brazil

Sergei, leader of team from Samara, Russia

Laura, leader of team from Hampton, UK

The Language Lab

A website project

Check-in

You are going to read about a young people's project to create an international website.

What websites do you use?
What do you use them for?
Have you ever sent anything for inclusion on a website?
List four additional reasons for visiting websites.

You are going to read a leaflet giving advice and guidance about creating a website.

Reading

- The leaflet **advises** the young people about working together in teams.
- It **suggests** to them how they should work.
- It **explains** who can help with any problems.

When did you last do an activity in a team?
What was it?

- These words are in the leaflet.

  access   respond   deadline   conference
  monitor   available   promptly

What do they mean? Check in a dictionary.

- Most of the teams live in different time zones.

What is a time zone? How many are there?

Looking at language

- Dictionary: **nouns**.
- Spelling: words ending *-tion / -sion*.
- Language development: **noun + noun**.

Grammar

- Practise **main tenses**: present simple, present continuous, past simple, past continuous.
- Practise **future**: *will*, *going to*, present perfect simple, present perfect continuous.
- Practise using *make* or *do*.

Writing

- Learn about the features of **writing to advise**.
- Write advice for a friend preparing for a family trip abroad.

Have you or anyone in your family ever travelled abroad? Where to?

- Write advice for a friend expecting a visitor from abroad.

Listening

- Laura, Ross, Jack and Holly's **conversation** about the four website project topics.
- Professor Brown's **explanation** of the teams and assignment of the topics.

Speaking

- Talk in a group about the topics.
- Tell the class about the topic you would like to work on.

The *www* project

Science · Art · Education · Environment

What's your experience of …?

What do you think about …?

Introducing the project …

You're going to create a young people's website with a worldwide perspective. Your task is to present your thoughts and ideas about the four subject areas, their role in your lives, now and in the future. You can include texts, photos, video, sound pictures, interviews, monologues – whatever you choose. When the website goes live, young people around the world will be able to access the material, respond to it and add to it. The website will grow from what you start.

Pairs of teams will create each subject area. You'll be assigned your area and your partner team in our first session. You can ask other teams for their views and information to help you develop your area and other teams will ask you to send information to them. This leaflet gives you advice about good working practices that you should try to use during the project.

Team leaders – important people!

You have already shown that you can work as a team. When you were doing your town projects, it was easy to meet up and co-ordinate your work. Now there will be eight of you working together and you could be on different sides of the world. Team leaders must play an essential role in project co-ordination.

Take me to your leader!

- Only team leaders should request information from another team. Requests from different team members for similar information could cause confusion and extra work.
- Make sure you copy your leader into emails that you send so that he or she knows what is going on.
- It's a good idea to hold regular review meetings and team leaders should organise these.

Working with your partner team

You'll have just one day in New York for discussion and planning – so make the most of it.

Hi, let's arrange a conference call for 10a.m.

- Plan thoroughly. Don't be afraid to change your plan later if it's not working out but do discuss it and do be aware of deadlines. At a certain point, it will be too late to make changes and you will have to stick with what you've got.
- Make sure you discuss the best ways of keeping in contact so you can go on developing your ideas for your part of the website.
- If you hold a video or phone conference, try to be there as a group so you all share in ideas and problem-solving.

Time zones

Remember that you all live in different parts of the world and in different time zones. Here's a chart that you can use to find out what time it is for the other teams.

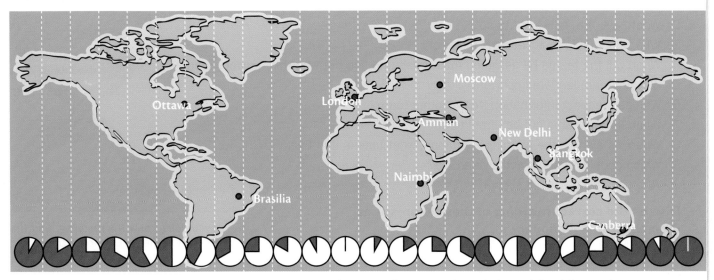

Use an appropriate form of contact at the right time – don't phone another team when it's the middle of their night.

What a nuisance! He's not answering.

Help is at hand

- Your project supervisor will monitor your progress and give you help and advice if you encounter difficulties or fall behind.
- Technical support is available from Georgi and the other design and maintenance staff of the project website.
- Remember to back everything up. You can't have too many copies of something, but you can have too few …

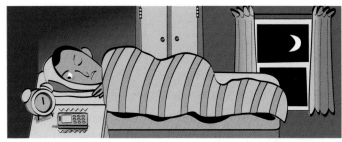

You have been making copies of everything, haven't you …?

Erm …

Handy hints box

- Do share information with your team – this is a group project.
- Don't go off doing your own thing – it's all about teamwork.
- Do try to respond to requests from other teams promptly. If you can't, contact them and fix a deadline that you can really make.
- Don't make changes to plans without talking to your partner team first.
- Do speak to your project supervisor if you find the workload too much – we're all here to help.
- Don't panic – there's a solution to every problem.
- Do enjoy it – make friends, make discoveries, have fun!

Good luck! You have several months to complete the work and then it will take several weeks to set up the website. When the website is launched, all the material you have created will be accessible all around the world!

Reading comprehension

1 Answer the questions.

1 What are the four subject areas?
2 What have the teams got to do?
3 Who will be able to access the material?
4 When will the teams be assigned their areas and find out who their partner team is?
5 Why are team leaders important?
6 Who can request information from another team?
7 What should teams not be afraid to do?
8 When it's eight in the morning in Amman, what time is it in England?
9 Which people can help and give advice?
10 Who can give technical support?

2 Discuss the correct meaning of these expressions then check in a dictionary.

1 make the most of it
  a to use a good situation to get the best possible result from it
  b to try to get more done than anyone else

2 stick with it
  a to glue something into position
  b to continue to use or do something and not change it

3 do your own thing
  a to do something with an object that belongs to you
  b do something that involves only yourself

If you don't know the meaning, find the expression in the text. Re-read the sentence then guess from the context.

3 Complete the sentences using the correct expression from Activity 2. Change the expression as necessary.

1 We don't see my cousin Anna at the weekend because she likes to _____.
2 I don't really like my new phone but it was expensive, so I'll _____.
3 It's going to be sunny this weekend, so let's _____ and go to the beach.

4 Discuss your answers to these questions.

1 What would be the best ways of keeping in touch with a team in another country?
2 Do you agree that it is important to have a leader for a group? Why? / Why not?
3 Why is it important to share information and not 'do your own thing'?
4 Why do you think you should not make changes to plans without talking to your partner team first?

Vocabulary check

Find these words in the leaflet on pages 8–9. Check any that you are not sure of in a dictionary.

co-ordinate essential request confusion deadline conference zone appropriate monitor encounter available maintenance back up go off promptly supervisor launch contact assign practice perspective respond thoroughly

Your views

- Which subject area would you be most interested in working on? Why?
- What media would you choose for your material? Explain your choices.
- Which advice in the leaflet would you find hardest to follow? Why?

A Dictionary work
Nouns

- **Nouns** in a dictionary are set out like this.

> **website** /ˈwebˌsaɪt/ *noun* [C] a place on the internet where information is available

- If a **noun** does not form its plural by adding only s, the **plural** is given.

> **copy** /ˈkɒpi/ (plural **copies**) *noun* [C] something that is exactly like something else

I **Look up these words and write whether they are countable or uncountable.**

1 task   2 advice   3 plan
4 progress   5 partner   6 information

2 **Choose two countable and two uncountable nouns from Activity I and use them in sentences of your own.**

B Spelling
Words ending in -tion / -sion

The endings **-tion** and **-sion** can be confusing.
- Most words end in **-tion** and sound /ʃən/.
  fiction   conjunction   addition

- There is a smaller group of nouns that end in **-sion**. Most of these come from verbs ending in **-d**, **-de** or **-se** and sound /ʃən/ or /ʒən/.
  verb = *comprehend*   noun = *comprehension*
  verb = *divide*   noun = *division*
  verb = *televise*   noun = *television*

I **Match the words in the box to the correct definitions.**

> multiplication   station   emigration
> discussion   possession   composition

1 the act of leaving your country to live somewhere else
2 a conversation about something important
3 4 x 6 = 24, for example
4 another word for an essay
5 where you would go to catch a train
6 something that you own

C Language development
noun + noun

- Two nouns can sometimes be put together to make a new word, e.g. *football, snowman.* These words are called **compound nouns.**

I **Think of two other examples.**

_____   _____

- Two nouns can sometimes be put together to make a phrase. Usually, the first noun tells you something about the second noun.
  road sign   a sign next to the road
  car tyre   a tyre for putting on a car

2 **Think of noun phrases for these objects.**

1 _____   2 _____

- Abstract nouns can be used in noun phrases.
  intelligence test   a test to find out how intelligent you are

3 **Think of noun phrases for these objects.**

beauty   danger

Look at these noun phrases from the leaflet you read. What do they mean?

phone conference   review meeting

Find two more examples of noun phrases in the leaflet. Discuss what they mean.

- More than two nouns can be put together. The first two nouns tell you about the third noun.

  intelligence test result
  the result of a test to find out how intelligent you are

- Noun phrases are useful because they can give you a lot of information in a few words. They are often used in newspaper headlines.

Diamond necklace theft

4 **What do you think the story was about?**

Grammar

1 **Read.**

A few months ago Laura, Ross, Jack and Holly **won** a competition. Their prize **was** a wonderful trip to New York. They **were looking forward** to it for weeks. When they **got** there, they **met** prize-winners from eight other countries. During their trip they **visited** museums and **went** to the theatre. One day, while they **were shopping** in a big department store, they **saw** a famous film star.

Today it is their final day of free time in New York and they **are sightseeing** for the last time. They **love** the city. Laura **is photographing** the skyscrapers. She always **takes** brilliant photos. Tomorrow morning they **are meeting** their new friends and Professor Brown. Professor Brown **wants** everyone to be there because he **has** an important announcement to make.

2 **Answer these questions.**

1 Why are the four friends in New York?
2 What happened when they arrived?
3 What are they doing now?
4 What do they think of New York?
5 Is Laura a good photographer? How do you know?
6 What are they doing tomorrow morning?

3 Remember!

Use the **present simple** for things that happen regularly.
Lucy phones her grandmother every week.
There are some verbs which are normally only used in the simple form, e.g. *like, love, hate, want, understand, remember, need, prefer, know, mean, sound, think* (have an opinion), *have* (possession).
Joe understands several languages.
Use the **present continuous** for things that are happening now.
At the moment they are visiting New York.
You can also use the present continuous for future events which are the result of plans or arrangements in the present.
Jane is taking her science exam next week.

Find examples of these uses of the present continuous and the present simple in the text.

4 **Answer these questions.**

1 Look around you. What's happening? Think of three sentences.
2 How do you and your friends spend your free time? Ask and then report back to the class.
3 What are your plans? What are you and your friends doing this evening? Tomorrow? Next week? Ask and report back to the class.

5 **Think of three questions to ask your friends using the present simple. Choose from these verbs:** *like, want, remember, need, know, think.* **Ask and answer. Report back to the class.**

6 Remember!

Use the **past simple** for actions which were completed in the past.
Jack and Laura flew to New York last week.
When they arrived, they went to their hotel.
Use the **past continuous** for actions which continued for some time in the past.
It was raining all morning.
You can use both tenses in one sentence. Use *while* or *when*.
While Joe was watching TV, the telephone rang.
Joe was watching TV when the telephone rang.

Find examples of these uses of the past simple and the past continuous in the text.

Meeting with Professor Brown

1

1 🎧 1.02 **Listen and read.**

Prof B: Hello, everyone. Come in, sit down and take one of these leaflets. Tell me, **have** you **enjoyed** your week in New York?

Holly: Oh, yes. It**'s been** absolutely brilliant.

Ross: We**'ve been sightseeing** and **taking** photos.

Prof B: And judging by all those bags, you**'ve been shopping**, too! Well, you've been here for a week and I know you**'ve made** lots of new friends.

Laura: Yes, we have.

Prof B: Next week you**'ll be** back home in your own countries but I know you**'re going to stay** in touch with each other because I'm giving you a job to do. You're **going to create** a website – a website where young people all over the world **will be able** to talk together and learn about each other's lives.

Laura: Wow! That sounds amazing!

Prof B: You**'ll find** more details in the leaflet that I**'ve** just **given** to you.

Jack: I **haven't seen** one yet. Where are they?

Prof B: There **has** never **been** a website like this before. It's a very exciting project …

2 **Answer these questions.**

1 What sort of week have the young people had?
2 How have they been spending their time?
3 Where will they be next week?
4 What are they going to create?
5 Why will the website be special?

> **Remember!**
>
> Use *will* + verb for actions which will happen in the future.
> *The concert **will take place** on Saturday.*
> Use *be going to* + verb.
> • when talking about plans and intentions.
>   *John **is going to be** a doctor.*
> • when a situation in the present means that an action is sure to happen in the future.
>   *Look at those black clouds! **It's going to rain**.*

3 **Find examples of *will* and *going to* in the dialogue.**

> **Remember!**
>
> We use the **present perfect simple:**
> • for actions that happened at an indefinite time in the past.
>   *My cousin **has been** to Australia.*
> • when something started in the past and still continues now.
>   *We **have lived** here for two years.*

> • when the result of a past action is visible now.
>   *Oh, no! I've **lost** my mobile!*
> We often use the present perfect simple with these words: *yet, just, ever, never*.
> *Have you **read** this book yet? Yes, I've **just** **finished** it.*
> *Has Joe **ever** been to America? No, he's **never** **been** there.*

4 **Find examples of the present perfect simple in the dialogue.**

> **Remember!**
>
> We use the **present perfect continuous:**
> • when an action started in the past and is still continuing now.
>   *Joe **has been playing** on his computer for hours.*
> • when the result of a past action is visible now and that action continued for some time.
>   *Lisa's eyes are red. I think she's **been crying**.*
> We often use a time phrase to show how long the action has been continuing.
> *… **since** 3 o'clock   … **for** a long time*

5 **Think of some more examples of the present perfect continuous like the first example above.**

> **Grammar extra p127**

Writing

Features of writing to advise

> Written instructions and written advice have some common features.

▶ **Introduction**

Make it clear what the advice is about.

> You're going to create a young people's website with a worldwide perspective.
> Your task is to present your thoughts and ideas about four subject areas.
> Pairs of teams will create each subject area.
> This leaflet gives you advice about good working practices ...

▶ **Layout**

The *www project* leaflet uses **sub-headings** to organise the advice.

> Team leaders – important people!   Working with your partner team

▶ **Imperative verbs**

> **Plan** thoroughly ...   **Remember** to back everything up ...

▶ **Precise language**

> request information   NOT 'have a chat'

> design and maintenance staff   NOT 'some people'

Other important features of written advice:

▶ **Personal / direct style**

Written advice appears to be talking directly to each individual reader by using the **second person**.

> **You** have already shown that **you** can work as a team.   Make sure **you** discuss ...   If **you** hold a video or phone conference ...

> ACTIVITY
>
> Change these third person sentences to **second person** sentences.
> 1 If she follows this advice, it should work.
> 2 He should not call his contact in the middle of the night.
> 3 They should not make changes to their plans without discussion.
> 4 He should make use of the technical support.
> 5 His supervisor will monitor his work and give him advice.

▶ **The language of advice**

The writer uses **imperative verbs** and **modal verbs** to suggest what you *must* or *should* do.

> Team leaders **must play** an essential role in project co-ordination.   Only team leaders **should request** information ...

> ACTIVITY
>
> Find some examples of **imperative verbs** in the leaflet.

The writer has also used language to **suggest** what you *might* do.

It's a good idea to hold regular review meetings …

if you hold a video or phone conference, **try to be** there as a group …

ACTIVITY

Use these **advice phrases** in sentences of your own.
1 It could be helpful …
2 You might like to …
3 An idea that could work …

Writing together

As a class you are going to write some advice **for a friend and their family on preparing for a trip. This is the first time they have done this.**

Things to think about.
Discuss their destination and the activities they will do there. Make notes.
- The most important thing to find out is the **destination**. Where are the family going on holiday? Are they staying in their country?
  Are they going abroad? Are they going somewhere very hot or very cold?
- How are they going to **travel**? By car / plane / train / ferry?
- You should also find out what they are going **to do** on holiday.
  Is it a lazy holiday on a beach?
  Is it an active holiday, such as skiing or pony trekking?

Discuss the items they will need to take with them. Make notes.
Their **destination**, how they are **travelling** and what they are going **to do** on holiday will affect the **documents** they need and **what they pack**. What **advice** would you give them about:

  passports currency insurance tickets baggage allowance
   clothes sun protection hand luggage last-minute checks

Look back at the information on the features of writing to advise.

Remember!
- Make it **clear** at the beginning what **the advice is about**.
- Use **sub-headings** to organise the advice.
- Use **imperative verbs** for things they must do.
- Use **the language of advice** for things they might do.
- Use a **personal style**.
- Use **precise language**.

Write your advice.

WB p10

Listening and speaking

Conversation practice

1 Laura, Ross, Jack and Holly are talking. Look at the photos and the words in the box. What are they talking about?

Science
Education
the Arts
the Environment
medicine
space travel
robots
the theatre
traditional music
renewable energy
wind farms
rainforests
endangered species

2 🎧 1.03 Listen to Laura, Ross, Jack and Holly. Were you right?

3 🎧 1.03 Read the phrases in the box. Listen again and spot the phrases.

*I bet   I wonder   fancy   You're joking   I'm not really into …
Absolutely   wait and see   keep our fingers crossed*

4 Imagine that you are taking part in the website project. Talk to your friends about the four topics. Use some of the phrases if you can.

Start like this: *What do you think about these topics? Which are the most interesting, do you think?*

Listening comprehension

1 🎧 1.04 Listen to Professor Brown. He is talking about the website project. He is telling the young people who they will be working with and which subject areas they will be responsible for.

2 🎧 1.04 Look at the chart. Listen again and fill in the chart.

	Countries	Subject area
Group 1		
Group 2		
Group 3		
Group 4		

Individual speaking

Imagine that you are going to take part in the website project. Which of Professor Brown's topics would you like to work on? WB p11

We ♥ New York

Check-in

Many cities are beautiful and interesting places. Sometimes they are crowded and noisy.

What sort of city do you think New York is?
What things do you think you can do there?
Would you like to go there? Why? / Why not?
List three things you would like to do in New York.

You are going to read some reviews and recounts written by the students.

Reading

- You are going to read the students' work before and after they corrected it.
- You are going to find the mistakes they missed.

What is the process of re-reading and correcting called?
The students make mistakes in three aspects of their writing. What do you think they are?

- These words are in the reviews you are going to read.
  fascinating amazing astonishing destroy evil

What do they mean? Check in a dictionary.

Looking at language

- Dictionary: **adjectives**.
- Spelling: *oi / oy.*
- Language development: **conjunction** *because.*

What does a conjunction do?

Grammar

- Learn about the **order of adjectives**.

What does an adjective do?

- Learn the use of ***see, hear, watch, feel something happen / happening***.
- Practise the meanings and use of **phrasal verbs with *come***.

Writing

- Learn about the features of **proofreading**.
- Proofread and correct a text.
- Proofread and rewrite two texts.

Listening

- Laura's **conversation** with her parents about her New York photos.
- Laura's **presentation** to her class about the Statue of Liberty.

Where in New York is the Statue of Liberty?

Speaking

- Talk with a partner about Laura's photos.
- Tell the class about two interesting buildings or sights in your town.

Reading 🎧 1.05
New York! New York!

The students have spent a wonderful, busy week in New York. They had spare time to see the sights of New York, and wrote some pieces for the 'About Us' section of the website based on what they saw and did.

Holly and Sofia visited the Metropolitan Museum of Art. They wrote about the experience but they made some spelling mistakes.

One of the most fasinating <u>plases</u> we visited in New York was the Metropolitan Museum of Art at 1000, 5th <u>Avenu</u> at 82nd Street – what an amazing <u>adress</u>!

We investigated the museum on the web to get some background information. It's one of the world's <u>larjest</u> art museums. It has more than two <u>milion</u> works of art from prehistory to the <u>presant</u> day, and the <u>exibits</u> come from all over the world. It opened its doors two the public on 13th April, 1870 and <u>neerly</u> five million <u>peple</u> visit it each year. Because it is so vast and there is so much to <u>sea</u>, we were given a floor plan. We were told it was a good idea to focus on three areas we really wanted to see. We chose the <u>secsions</u> on Islamic Art, Chinese Art and Arms and Armour. We made <u>shure</u> we had some time left at the end of the visit to go up to the roof garden which has a <u>grate</u> view of Central Park.

They proofread what they had written by underlining the words they weren't sure of and checking in a dictionary.

One of the most fasinating places we visited in New York was the Metropolitan Museum of Art at 1000, 5th Avenue at 82nd Street – what an amazing address!

We investigated the museum on the web to get some background information. It's one of the world's largest art museums. It has more than two million works of art from prehistory to the present day, and the exhibits come from all over the world. It opened its doors two the public on 13th April, 1870 and nearly five million people visit it each year. Because it is so vast and there is so much to see, we were given a floor plan. We were told it was a good idea to decide on three areas we really wanted to see. We chose the sections on Islamic Art, Chinese Art and Arms and Armour. We made sure we had some time left at the end of the visit to go up to the roof garden that has a great view of Central Park.

Did they find all their spelling mistakes?

Jack and Ali were in a group of students who went to the theatre in Times Square. They wrote about the visit but they made some grammatical mistakes.

You can't go to New York and not <u>seen</u> a Broadway musical. Our group decided <u>about</u>
The Lion King at the Lyceum Theatre in Times Square.
We <u>take</u> a train to 42nd Street and arrived in 'Theatre Land'. It <u>were</u> after dark but you would
never have guessed it. So many people! So <u>much</u> lights from so many billboards. One <u>was</u> even powered by wind
and solar energy! We watched the lights flashing on and off as we queued for our tickets.
And what about the show? Magical. Prince Simba <u>are</u> first in line to the throne but his evil uncle, Scar, <u>plot</u>
to destroy King Mufasa and Simba. Scar brings about Mufasa's death, then <u>convince</u> young prince Simba that
it was his fault. Simba doesn't <u>knows</u> the truth and he runs away since many
years. When Simba discovers the truth, he returns home and becomes King. The
extraordinary, huge, vivid animal costumes <u>was</u> astonishing. The audience booed
Scar and cheered Simba. Everyone <u>were</u> humming and singing as they left the
theatre.
Back in Times Square – just as bright and noisy as when we arrived. No
wonder New York is called 'the city that never <u>sleep</u>'!

They proofread what they had written and corrected the mistakes they found.

You can't go to New York and not see a Broadway musical. Our group decided on
The Lion King at the Lyceum Theatre in Times Square.
We took a train to 42nd Street and arrived in 'Theatre Land'. It was after dark but you would never
have guessed it. So many people! So many lights from so many billboards. One is even powered by
wind and solar energy! We watched the lights flashing on and off as we queued for our tickets.
And what about the show? Magical. Prince Simba are first in line to the throne but his evil uncle,
Scar, plots to destroy King Mufasa and Simba. Scar brings about Mufasa's death, then convinces
young prince Simba that it was his fault. Simba doesn't know the truth and he runs away since many
years. When Simba discovers the truth, he returns home and becomes King. The extraordinary,
huge, vivid animal costumes were astonishing. The audience booed Scar and cheered
Simba. Everyone were humming and singing as they left the theatre.
Back in Times Square – just as bright and noisy as when we arrived. No wonder
New York is called 'the city that never sleeps'!

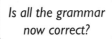

Is all the grammar now correct?

Laura drafted a short piece about meeting Professor Brown at the end of their week in New York. Laura made some mistakes with her punctuation. She proofread what she had written and highlighted parts where she thought she had made mistakes.

Professor Brown inquired if we had enjoyed our week in New York. Holly said Its been absolutely brilliant We told him that we had been sightseeing taking photos and shopping.
He went on to say that we would soon be back in our own country's but we needed to stay in touch because we had a task to perform. "What sort of task? Jack asked.
the Professor informed us that "We are going to create a website where young people can learn about each others' lives." He told us to take a leaflet where wed find more information about the project,

Professor Brown inquired if we had enjoyed our week in New York. Holly said, "It's been absolutely brilliant We told him that we had been sightseeing, taking photos and shopping.
He went on to say that we would soon be back in our own countries, but we needed to stay in touch because we had a task to perfom. "What sort of task?" Jack asked.
The Professor informed us that we are going to create a website where young people can learn about each others' lives. He told us to take a leaflet where we'd find more information about the project.

Is any punctuation still missing?

Reading comprehension

I Answer these questions.

1 Where did Holly and Sofia visit while they were in New York?
2 What was the address?
3 a How many works of art has it?
   b How many people visit each year?
4 What could they see from the roof garden?
5 Where was *The Lion King* showing?
6 How are Scar and Simba related?
7 What differences did Jack and Ali notice in Times Square before and after the performance?
8 What three things did the students tell Professor Brown they had been doing?
9 What was the job Professor Brown gave them to do?
10 Where would they find more information?

2 Discuss the correct meaning of these expressions as they are used in the passages and then check in a dictionary.

1 investigated   a looked at the top of something
                 b used a book or a computer to find information
2 made sure   a took the action that was necessary for something to happen
                 b was certain that something was real
3 first in line a at the beginning
                 b before anyone else

3 Can you find …

1 the two spelling mistakes Holly and Sofia didn't spot?
2 the three grammatical mistakes Jack and Ali missed?
3 the two punctuation mistakes Laura didn't correct?

4 Discuss the answers to these questions.

1 For how many years has the museum been open?
2 How do you know that Jack and Ali's group went to an evening performance?
3 What evidence can you find that the audience enjoyed the performance?
4 Look at Laura's first draft with all the punctuation mistakes. What mark would you give it out of ten?

Vocabulary check

Find these words in the passages on pages 18–19. Check any you are not sure of in a dictionary.

fascinating   prehistory   exhibits   floor plan   billboards   solar   vivid   sightseeing   create

Your views

● Would you be interested in visiting the Metropolitan Museum of Art? Why? / Why not?
● Why do you think proofreading your work before you hand it in is important?
● Do you think having an 'About Us' section on the website is a good idea? Why? / Why not?

A Dictionary work
Adjectives

- **Adjectives** in a dictionary are set out like this.

> **wonderful** /ˈwʌndəfl/ *adjective* extremely good

- If there is a spelling change for the **comparative** and **superlative**, these forms are given.

> **busy** /ˈbɪzi/ (**busier, busiest**) *adjective* having lots of things to do

1 **Look up these adjectives and write their comparatives.**

| 1 noisy | 2 sad | 3 lonely |
| 4 hot | 5 lovely | 6 lucky |

2 **Look up these adjectives and write their superlatives.**

| 1 wet | 2 gloomy | 3 dry |
| 4 thin | 5 heavy | 6 shiny |

B Spelling
oi and oy

In some words **oi** and **oy** make the sound /ɔɪ/.

*Back in Times Square – just as **noisy** and bright as when we arrived.*

*… his evil uncle plots to **destroy** King Mufasa and Simba.*

- **oi** is usually used in the middle of a word.
  sp**oi**l ch**oi**ce
- **oy** is usually used at the end of a word.
  b**oy** enj**oy**
- **oy** is used in the middle of a word when it is followed by a vowel.
  r**oy**al s**oy**a

1 **Add *oi* or *oy* to each word.**

1 t ___ ___	2 ___ ___ l	3 j ___ ___ n
4 v___ ___age	5 av___ ___d	6 v___ ___ce
7 empl ___ ___	8 c ___ ___ n	9 l ___ ___al

2 **Use five of the words in sentences of your own.**

C Language development
Conjunction *because*

- A **conjunction** joins two main clauses.

- The conjunction *because* is used to join two ideas and to give a reason for something.
  a *They went to New York. They had won a competition.*
  b *They went to New York **because** they had won a competition.*

1 **Which clause in b tells you the final action? Which clause in b tells you the reason for the action?**

- Usually, *because* comes in the middle of the sentence but it can also come at the beginning. ***Because** the museum is so vast and there is so much to see, we were given a floor plan.*

2 **Which clause tells you the final action? Which clause tells you the reason for the action?**

- Remember that *because* introduces the reason. A reason clause that begins with *because* is not a sentence by itself. It needs the final, completed action to make a complete sentence.

3 **Which of these is a complete sentence?**

Because the bus arrived extremely late
Because it rained, we went home

Think of an ending to the incomplete sentence. The reason clause can be long. Which of these is a complete sentence?

Because there were dark clouds like black curtains hanging in the sky and it was starting to rain
Because it was late and the TV programme about cars was extremely uninteresting, I went to bed

Think of an ending for the incomplete sentence.

- If a long sentence starts with *Because* and is hard to understand, find the clause with the complete action. Then read the *Because* clause again.
- If a comprehension test asks for a short answer, it does not have to be a complete sentence. You can begin your answer with *because*, e.g.
  Why did Laura take lots of photos?
  Because she liked the city so much.
- If the test asks you to answer in complete sentences, you must include the clause that gives the action.

Answer the question about Laura in a complete sentence.

Watch out!

Grammar

1 **Read.**

Laura, Ross, Jack and Holly and all the other students have had a **wonderful, busy** week in New York. They've loved the **noisy, bustling** streets, the **yellow** taxis and, of course, the **incredible, tall** skyscrapers. One afternoon they visited the Metropolitan Museum of Art. In the Arms and Armour section they were fascinated by **extraordinary, ancient, metal** suits of armour. In the **Chinese** section they admired **beautiful, embroidered, silk** robes.

One evening they went to Times Square. They were surprised by the bright lights of the **colourful advertising** billboards. Some were powered by **wind and solar** energy. At the Lyceum Theatre they saw a production of *The Lion King*. They loved the **fantastic, huge, vivid** costumes worn by the actors.

2 **Correct these sentences about the text above.**

1 They loved the quiet, bustling streets of New York.
2 At the museum they were bored by modern, metal suits of armour.
3 They admired beautiful, painted, silk robes from Japan.
4 They loved the bright, flashing lights in Central Park.
5 Some of the billboards were powered by wind and water energy.
6 At the theatre they enjoyed the fantastic, tiny, vivid costumes.

3 **Remember!**

When **adjectives** precede the noun, they usually appear in this order:
opinion + size + age + shape
a **beautiful, big** book (opinion + size)
a **tall, young** man (size + age)
an **old, rectangular** mirror (age + shape)
strange, little, round holes (opinion + size + shape)

Put the adjectives in front of the nouns in the correct order.

1 a castle (ancient, amazing)
2 a holiday (marvellous, long)
3 a box (round, tiny)
4 a lady (old, little)
5 a window (new, oval)
6 a painting (triangular, unusual)
7 a pool (huge, extraordinary, circular)

4 **Remember!**

Other adjectives usually appear in this order, after listing opinion, size, age and shape: colour + origin + material + purpose
black, Russian bears (colour + origin)
a **Chinese, silk** shawl (origin + material)
a **metal coat** hook (material + purpose)
brown, leather riding boots
(colour + material + purpose)

Put at least two adjectives in front of the nouns. Choose words from the box. There are many possible combinations!

scarlet   yellow   purple   grey   colourful   New York
Italian   African   wooden   woollen   leather
glass   advertising   racing   walking   dancing

1 shoes   2 a vase   3 a taxi   4 billboards
5 a car   6 elephants   7 gloves   8 a stick

5 **Describe these pictures. Use two or three adjectives in front of nouns.**

Remember!

The order of adjectives in front of nouns:
opinion + size + age + shape + colour + origin + material + purpose

Meeting:
UK, Australia,
Russia

1 🔊 1.06 **Listen and read.**

Sergei: We've got the best topic by far – in my opinion anyway.

Laura: I was really hoping we'd get the Environment. I had my fingers crossed!

Carrie: So did I! I was so happy when Professor Brown announced it!

Ross: **I saw** your face **light up** when he gave the Environment to our group.

Laura: I **heard** you **whispering** to Sergei. You seemed pretty excited.

Carrie: I was saying that we should do a feature on the Great Barrier Reef.

Sergei: Carrie does scuba diving so she knows a lot about the reef.

Ross: I came across an article about it recently. It said that scientists **have noticed** the coral **dying**.

Laura: That's terrible! Is it true?

Carrie: I'm afraid so. The coral is dying in some places.

Sergei: Oh, there's so much we can write about!

Ross: Climate change – that's having a terrible effect on the Arctic.

Laura: The destruction of the rainforests – that's really important.

Sergei: Renewable sources of energy – wind power, tidal power, that sort of thing.

Carrie: Ooh! I can **feel** this website **growing** already!

2 Answer these questions.

1 Where is Carrie from? How about Sergei? And Ross and Laura?

2 Is Carrie excited about their topic? How do you know?

3 How does Carrie know about the Great Barrier Reef?

4 What have scientists noticed about the reef?

5 Why does Carrie say, "I can feel this website growing already."?

6 What do they want to feature on their section of the website?

3 Find the correct endings to these sentences. Choose from the phrases in the box.

> take a photo   shout her name   light up
> steal the diamond   start the engine   shake

1 Ross saw Carrie's face …
   Ross saw Carrie's face light up.

2 Holly heard someone …

3 I saw Laura …

4 Did you see the thief …?

5 It was an earthquake! We felt the ground …

6 I heard the driver …

4 Ask and answer as in the example. Use verb + noun + present participle.

1 What could you hear? (rain – fall – roof)
   I could hear the rain falling on the roof.

2 What did you see? (lights – flash – darkness)

3 What could the boy smell? (meat – roast – oven)

4 What did they watch? (snow – fall – sky)

5 What did the tourists feel? (sun – burn – skin)

5 Read the pairs of sentences and explain the difference in meaning.

1 I heard someone shout my name.
   I heard someone shouting my name.

2 I saw the girl wave goodbye.
   I saw the girl waving goodbye.

3 I felt an insect bite my arm.
   I felt an insect biting my arm.

Remember!

After **verbs of perception** (*see, hear, feel, smell*, etc.):

- use the infinitive (without *to*) for short, sudden or completed actions.
  *She **heard** the balloon **burst**.*

- use the present participle for longer, continuing actions.
  *He could **feel** the water **rising**.*

Grammar extra p127 ▶

Writing

Features of proofreading

> **Proofreading is checking your work for** mistakes **in spelling, grammar and punctuation.**

▶ Spelling

You should always use a dictionary to check your **spelling** if:
- the word you have written doesn't 'look' right
- you are using a difficult word that you do not normally use.

> **ACTIVITY**
>
> Each of these sentences has one **spelling** mistake. Correct the mistakes.
> 1 We were told to be sensable when we visited the museum.
> 2 It was very peacefull on the roof garden.
> 3 I beleive *The Lion King* is the best musical I've ever seen.
> 4 Times Square at night is amazeing.
> 5 We were siting quietly waiting for Professor Brown to arrive.

▶ Grammar

It is often helpful to read aloud what you have written. You can often 'hear' when your **grammar** is incorrect.

> **ACTIVITY**
>
> Each of these sentences has one **grammar** mistake. Correct the mistakes.
> 1 The theatre trip were very enjoyable.
> 2 Whose going to be the leader of the group?
> 3 We had a opportunity to go shopping in New York.
> 4 I have been in New York since three days.
> 5 Professor Brown doesn't wants us to lose touch.

▶ Punctuation

Always check that you have:
- put in capital letters and full stops
- used commas in lists
- finished questions with a question mark
- used apostrophes in contractions
- used apostrophes to show ownership
- used speech marks for direct speech.

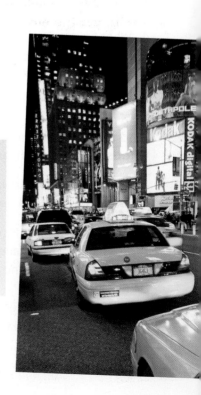

> **ACTIVITY**
>
> Each of these sentences has one **punctuation** mistake. Correct the mistakes.
> 1 the Metropolitan Museum is one of the largest in the world.
> 2 We went to sections on Islamic Art Chinese Art Arms and Armour and the roof garden.
> 3 The theatre groups visit was very enjoyable.
> 4 Times Square was so crowded said Ross.
> 5 "Are you looking forward to going home." asked Laura

Writing together

Laura wrote an email to her family after she had been on a bus tour of New York. She typed very quickly and made some mistakes. As a class, proofread what she wrote and correct the mistakes.

1 **Proofread Laura's email.**

To	Mum and Dad
From	Laura
Subject	New York! New York!

Professor Brown said that the best way to get the 'feel' of a sity was to take a bus tour. We saw so many places, I'm sure I cant remember half of them. Central Park is huge The tour guide told us it covers 843 acres! The bus took us along the Hudson River and we could see the Statue of Liberty in the distance. I hope I get a chance to see it close up on the ferry. The Empire State Building is on 34th Street. It were the tallest building in the world for 40 years but there's a biger one in Dubai now. We passed the Metropolitan Museum of Art that Professor Brown says we should visit, and we saw some very famus shops – Macys Bloomingdales and Saks on 5th Avenue. We got off the bus at Times Square were all the theatres are and walk back to the hotel.

Tomorrow, we can choose where we wants to go. Im going on the ferry to the Statue of Liberty and Ellis Island. The island are where all imigrants to America between 1892 and 1954 passed through and were registered. It says in the guidebook that it dealt with 10,000 immigrants a day! Can you believe that.

The other people that are here are really great. I've made new friends from all sorts of different countrys. It is really intresting finding out about where they comes from. Everyone is having a good time. I will write again soon.

You are looking for five spelling mistakes, five grammatical mistakes and five punctuation mistakes.

2 **Write out the email without mistakes.**

WB p19

Conversation practice

1 **Laura is back home in Hampton in the UK. She is talking to her mum and dad. Look at the photos and the words in the box. What do you think they are talking about?**

> *Central Park   5th Avenue   Times Square*
> *Metropolitan Museum of Art   Empire State Building*

2 🎧 **Listen to Laura talking with her mum and dad. Were you right?**

3 🎧 **Read the phrases in the box. Listen again and spot the phrases.**

> *for ages   loads of stuff   absolutely massive   No chance!*
> *Good heavens!   no doubt   What a pity!*

4 **Talk with your friends about Laura's photos. Try to remember as much detail as you can. Use some of the phrases if you can.**

   Start like this: *Look at these photos of New York. They're great, aren't they?*

Listening comprehension

1 🎧 **Listen to Laura. She is at school and she is giving a talk to her class about the Statue of Liberty.**

2 🎧 **Read the questions. Listen again and answer the questions.**

   1 Where does the Statue of Liberty stand?
   2 When does it date from?
   3 Where was it made?
   4 What does the statue depict?
   5 How do you reach the statue?
   6 How tall is the statue in total?
   7 Which part of the statue can you visit?
   8 How do you get there?

3 **Talk about the Statue of Liberty.**

Individual speaking

Choose two interesting sights (buildings, monuments, etc.) in your town. Talk to the class about them.

WB p20

Different places

Check-in

When you read a story set in a country different to your own, you will come across cultural details that you have never heard of before and, sometimes, words from another language.

> *What is 'culture'?*
> *How could you find out the meaning of a word from another language?*
> *What aspects of your own culture do you think might be different to the culture of other countries in the world? List three things.*

You are going to read a story about a girl who has to move to Africa to live with her grandmother.

Reading

- The girl's name is Martine and she comes from England.

> *Think of three things that she would find different in Africa.*

- The setting of the story is an African wildlife reserve.
- These words are in the story you are going to read.
  carnivore   chorus   horizon   drench   blindly

> *What do they mean? Check in a dictionary.*

Looking at language

- Dictionary: **verbs**.
- Spelling: **gh** sounding **/f/**; **silent gh**.
- Language development: **conjunctions; sentences with more than two main clauses; suffix** -ness

> *List four conjunctions.*

Grammar

- Practise the **past perfect simple** and **past perfect continuous**.
- Practise **so (that), in order to**.
- Practise **phrasal verbs with set**.

> *Think of one phrasal verb using* set.

Writing

- Learn about the features of **stories from other cultures**.
- Write a story about travel in your own country, expressing cultural features.
- Write a story set in your school, including cultural features.

Listening

- Jack and Laura's **conversation** about photos of Australia.
- Carrie's **interview** with Professor Donovan about the Great Barrier Reef.

> *Where is the Great Barrier Reef?*

Speaking

- Talk with a partner about the photos of Australia.
- Tell the class about a place of great natural beauty or importance.

The White Giraffe

Martine Allen's parents have died and she has travelled from England to Africa to live with her grandmother who owns a wildlife reserve. Tendai, a Zulu tracker who works for her grandmother, has told her of a rare white giraffe believed to be in the reserve. He has found its tracks and he has followed them but he has never been lucky enough to see the animal itself. One rainy night, Martine glimpses the giraffe from her bedroom window. She decides to go into the reserve to find it.

The air was perfume-sweet with the scent of fallen mangoes and gardenia blossoms. Martine set off blindly through the dripping trees in the general direction of the game park gate. The one useful thing she'd overheard during her investigations the previous week had been Tendai telling her grandmother the new code for the padlock. She'd made a point of committing the numbers to memory. When her hands touched the cold metal gate, she felt for the heavy chain that bound it and the lock that secured it. Only then did she switch on her torch and enter the numbers on the wet dial. The padlock clicked open! Martine stared down at it, unable to believe that it had been so easy. She realised that she'd been secretly hoping all along that something would happen to prevent her from going into the game reserve. She glanced over her shoulder. Once more, the house stood in darkness. Whatever happened now, there was no turning back.

Martine stepped through the gate and stifled a cry of terror. Two red eyes glared at her. The bushes shook violently and a waterbuck sprang up so close to Martine that its fur actually brushed her. With a shake of its horns, it bounded away into the blackness.

Martine's heart smacked wildly against her ribcage. She tried to imagine what Tendai would do in a similar situation. Not that he was likely to be in a similar situation, but if he were she was sure that everything would be about staying calm and thinking clearly. "Focus," she thought. "I have to focus. I can do this."

More than anything in the world she wanted to find the white giraffe. Why, she wasn't sure; she just knew she had to do it …

The beam from the torch picked out the path that led down to the waterhole, where the frogs were competing in a noisy chorus. Blue lightning shuddered over the mountains on the far horizon. Martine set off as quickly as she dared, trying to avoid the puddles. Even so, her jeans were soon soaked through. In places the grass was taller than she was and cold droplets drenched her hair and ran down her neck.

As she walked, unseen creatures slithered and scurried and hopped away through the undergrowth. Martine tried not to imagine the worst. She wasn't sure which she was most scared of, snakes and creepy-crawlies or man-eating carnivores, but she fervently hoped that she didn't meet any of them. After what seemed an age, the temperature dropped and she saw she'd reached the water's edge. She tried to pinpoint the exact spot where she had seen the giraffe. She was pretty sure it had been beside the old gum tree that stood, like a startled skeleton, on the left bank of the waterhole.

As if sensing danger, the frogs fell silent. Tendrils of mist hovered over the water and the night air was laden with threat. Martine quelled the butterflies in her stomach. She'd come too far to go back now. She lifted her torch and shone it into the surrounding bush. Nothing moved. Not a mouse, not a lion, not even a bird. Disappointment hit her like a blow. What had she been thinking? A mythical giraffe! She'd risked her life in pursuit of a fairy tale and now she had to try to get home in one piece.

Sheer instinct warned Martine something was behind her. The same sixth sense told her to turn around very, very slowly. A Cape cobra was coiled in the mud barely six feet away from her, hood spread wide, swaying in the yellow torch light. Martine recognised it immediately as one of the most poisonous snakes in Africa, more deadly even than the mamba. Its golden colouring was unmistakable. So was the band around its throat.

The cobra's lips parted and its black tongue flickered out evilly. Martine dropped her torch in panic. It rolled behind a boulder and dimmed to a faint glow.

Then it went out.

In the split second before she was plunged into darkness, Martine saw the cobra draw back its head to strike. Helplessly, she waited for its lethal bite.

It never came. Instead, a pale blur exploded from the trees. There was a hideous hissing sound and the flash of flying hooves. The last thing Martine saw before she crumpled to the ground was the white giraffe.

from The White Giraffe *by Lauren St John*

Glossary

Zulu:	a south African tribe
mango:	a fruit
gardenia:	a flowering plant
waterhole:	a small lake
waterbuck:	an animal like a deer
gum:	a kind of tree
cobra:	a kind of snake
mamba:	an extremely poisonous kind of snake

Reading comprehension

I Read the statements. Write T (true) or F (false).

1 A chain with a padlock bound and secured the gate into the game reserve. ___

2 It was not easy to open the padlock. ___

3 The waterbuck bounded away into the blackness. ___

4 Martine got drenched as she walked towards the waterhole. ___

5 She was more scared of snakes than creepy-crawlies. ___

6 Martine was disappointed because the giraffe was not at the waterhole. ___

7 Her sixth sense told her not to turn round quickly. ___

8 The cobra had golden bands around its throat. ___

9 Martine dropped her torch behind a boulder. ___

10 The cobra was about to strike when the white giraffe came out from the trees. ___

2 Read these phrases. Write the correct phrase next to each meaning.

> fairy tale   sixth sense   split second
> pretty sure   butterflies in your stomach

You know most of the words in the phrases. Work out what each complete phrase means.

1 a very short period of time _____

2 a feeling of nervousness _____

3 a traditional story about things that do not happen in real life _____

4 a feeling that people sometimes have that tells them something _____

5 fairly certain _____

3 Discuss the answers to these questions.

1 Was Martine scared of going into the reserve? How do you know?

2 Why do you think she wants to find the white giraffe more than anything in the world?

3 What sort of personality do you think Martine has?

4 What do you think happened at the end of this part of the story?

4 Read these words from the story. Find them in the text. Discuss their meanings.

> pinpoint   padlock   undergrowth
> creepy-crawlies   droplet   overhear   ribcage

Looking for words within a word can help you to work out the meaning.

Vocabulary check

Find these words in the text. Write the word class for each list. Check any words you are not sure of in a dictionary.

1 _____ blow blur carnivore chain chorus code dial hoof horizon instinct
   investigation panic perfume puddle reserve skeleton tendril throat

2 _____ bind commit dare drench drip focus prevent quell risk secure stifle

3 _____ laden lethal mythical previous sheer

4 _____ barely blindly fervently

Your views

- How would you feel if you had to go and live in a completely different country with a different culture? Why?
- Do you think living on a game reserve would be an adventure? Why? / Why not?
- Is there anything you would be scared of?

Looking at language

A Dictionary work
Verbs

> • **Verbs** in a dictionary are set out like this. The **infinitive** form is used.
>
> > **walk** /wɔːk/ *verb* [I] to move forward by putting one foot in front of the other
>
> • If there is a spelling change for some tenses, these **tenses** are given.
>
> > **step** /step/ (**steps, stepping, stepped**) *verb* [I] to move somewhere by putting one foot in front of the other
>
> • If a verb has an **irregular past tense**, this tense is given.
>
> > **see** /siː/ (**sees, seeing, saw**) *verb* [I/T] to notice something or someone with your eyes

1 **Look up these verbs and write the past tense of each.**
1 carry   2 drop   3 dry   4 stop

2 **Write whether these verbs are transitive or intransitive.**
1 swirl   2 contain
3 cover   4 trudge
5 chirp   6 capture

> If a verb is transitive, it has an object: **I ate the apple**. If a verb is intransitive it has no object. **I ate slowly.**

3 **Use one transitive and one intransitive verb from Activity 1 in sentences of your own.**

I ate slowly.

B Spelling
gh words

> • Sometimes **gh** makes the sound /f/.
> … he had never been lucky **enough** to see the animal itself.
> • When **gh** is followed by **t**, the **gh** is **silent**.
> "Focus," she **thought** …

1 **Read these words. Write ƒ or *silent* for the sound the gh makes in each of them.**
1 rough _____   2 right _____   3 laugh _____
4 naughty _____   5 cough _____   6 tough _____
7 straight _____   8 trough _____

2 **Write the past tense of these verbs.**
1 catch   2 buy   3 fight   4 think

C Language development
Joining two main clauses with a conjunction

> *Remember that a main clause can be a sentence on its own.*

> • You have learned about joining two main clauses with the **conjunctions** *and*, *but* and *or*.
> I go to City School **and** my sister goes there, too.
> Our school is large **but** it's a friendly place.
> We can go to school by bus **or** we can go by train.

> *These joined main clauses are called compound sentences.*

Sentences with more than two main clauses with conjunctions

> • Sentences can contain more than two main clauses joined by conjunctions.
> He has found its tracks **and** he has followed them **but** he has never been lucky enough to see the animal itself.

1 **Read the three sentences. Rewrite them as one sentence joining them with two different conjunctions.**

> *Remember! Usually, you should avoid joining three main clauses using and both times.*

1 Martine looked out of the window. She saw the white giraffe. It was only for a moment.
2 Martine stepped through the gate. She saw that she could turn right. She could turn left.

2 **Read each set of three short sentences then the longer sentence you have written. Discuss how they are different.**

Word building: suffix -ness

> • Some adjectives can be made into nouns by adding -ness e.g.
> Once more, the house stood in **darkness**.

3 **Write *kind, happy* and *careless* as nouns.**

Grammar

1 | Read.

Martine set off towards the game park gate. The previous week she **had overheard** Tendai telling her grandmother the new code for the padlock. She **had made** a point of remembering it. When she reached the gate, she entered the numbers on the padlock and it clicked open. Martine stared down at it, unable to believe that it **had been** so easy. She realised that she **had been** secretly **hoping** that something would happen to prevent her from going into the game reserve.

Martine made her way towards the waterhole. After what seemed an age, she saw she **had reached** the water's edge. She tried to pinpoint the spot where she **had seen** the giraffe. The animal was not there. What **had** she **been thinking**? She **had risked** her life in pursuit of a fairy tale.

2 Answer these questions.

1 How did Martine know the code for the padlock?
2 Why was Martine surprised when the padlock opened?
3 What did she realise after 'what seemed an age'?
4 What did she try to pinpoint?
5 Had she been thinking clearly when she set off that night?
6 What had she done?

3 Choose the correct endings. Write the letters.

1 Martine was able to open the padlock … _____
2 She was surprised that … _____
3 It was Tendai … _____
4 She went to the waterhole … _____
5 She was angry with herself … _____

a because she had put her life in danger.
b where she had seen the white giraffe.
c because she had found out the code.
d who had first told her about the giraffe.
e opening the padlock had been so easy.

4 Complete these sentences with the words in brackets. Use the past perfect continuous.

1 Before Martine came to Africa, she …
   (live – England)
   Before Martine came to Africa, she had been living in England.
2 She remembered that the giraffe …
   (stand – waterhole)
3 Sam thought back to his holiday. Last week …
   (lie – sunny beach)

4 Ann was disappointed with her exam results. She … (hope – higher mark)
5 The detective questioned the suspects. What … (do – 9 o'clock last night)?
6 Joe asked the teacher to repeat the question. He … (not – pay attention)

5 Read the sentences and think of possible explanations. What had happened or what had been happening previously? Work in pairs then share your ideas with the class.

1 Joe's clothes were soaking wet. Why?
   Perhaps he had fallen in the river.
   Or: Maybe he had been walking in the rain.
2 Lucy was furious with her brother. Why?
3 The teacher praised the students. Why?
4 The tourists were exhausted. Why?
5 Jimmy was late for school. Why?

Remember!

We use the **past perfect simple** for an action which happened **before** another action in the past.
*She put on her silver necklace. Her mother **had given** it to her on her eighteenth birthday.*
*After Harry **had revised** for two hours, he took a break.*

We use the **past perfect continuous**:
* when an earlier past action continued for some time.
   *When I met Joe, he **had been living** in Paris for two years.*
* when an earlier past action had been happening around a certain point in the past.
   *Lucy tried to remember the previous day's events. At one o'clock she **had been having** lunch.*

Meeting:
4pm
Jack and Laura's house

1 🔊 **1.10** **Listen and read.**

Holly: Oh, look! We've got an email from Carrie.

Jack: There are a couple of attachments, too.

Laura: You're in the way, Jack! Move, **so** we can all see the screen.

Holly: She says she's attached some photos **so that** we can see what happens to a reef when the coral dies.

Ross: And she's got the name of an expert at Brisbane University. She's going to interview him **in order to** find out more.

Laura: Did you see that article about rainforests in the newspaper? It says vast areas of forest are destroyed every day **so that** farmers have land where they can grow crops.

Jack: The rainforests are cleared to provide land for cattle, too.

Holly: We should email Sofia in Brazil **to** ask her about this.

Jack: The trees are cut down just **so** we can eat meat.

Laura: You're going to become a vegetarian, are you, Jack? No more burgers?

Jack: Well, …

2 Answer these questions.

1 What has just arrived?
2 How many attachments are there?
3 Why did Carrie send some photos?
4 Who is Carrie going to interview? Why?
5 Why are large parts of the rainforest cut down? Give two reasons.
6 Why are they going to email Sofia?

3 Choose the correct endings. Write the letters.

1 Laura asked Jack to move … _____
2 Jack said that the forests are destroyed … _____
3 Martine went into the game park … _____
4 She shone her torch on to the padlock … _____
5 Harry decided not to go to the cinema … _____
6 I'm going to give you my email address … _____

a so he could revise for his English exam.
b so that she could see the dial.
c so that we can stay in touch.
d so that she could find the rare giraffe.
e so they could all see the screen.
f just so people can eat meat.

4 Ask and answer in pairs. Find the answers in the box. Use *to* or *in order to*.

> discover more about the Great Barrier Reef   buy souvenirs   find the white giraffe   create a young people's website   find out more about the destruction of the rainforests   see where she was going   make space for farming and cattle   go to the theatre

1 Why did Martine go into the game park?
She went into the game park to (OR: in order to) find the white giraffe.

2 Why did she shine her torch along the path?

3 Why is Carrie going to interview a university professor?

4 Why are they going to email Sofia?

5 Why have vast areas of the rainforest been cut down?

6 Why did the group go to Times Square in New York?

7 Why did Holly go to the department stores on 5th Avenue?

8 Why are all the students working together?

Remember!

There are several ways to express the **idea of purpose or intention**.

so + clause
*Give me your number **so** I can phone you.*
*Take a book **so that** you can read on the train.*

to + infinitive OR *in order to* + infinitive
*He went to Paris **to** learn French.*
*She went to the river **in order to** see the giraffe.*

5 Find examples of these constructions in the dialogue.

➤ Grammar extra p127

Features of stories from other cultures

> When we read stories that are set in different parts of the world, we are reading about another culture. Some of the details in the story will be quite normal for the characters, but quite unusual for the reader.
>
> Stories are usually written in past tenses and can be in the first or third person. Stories have three main features.

▶ **Plot**

What **happens** in a story is called the **plot**.

The extract from *The White Giraffe* is about Martine going into the game reserve.

It begins with Martine leaving the house.

> **ACTIVITY**
>
> What **happens** next?
>
> 1 How does she get into the game reserve?
>
> 2 What happens up to the moment she sees the white giraffe?

▶ **Setting**

The **setting** is **where** the story takes place.

The writer uses **description** so that the reader can imagine where the character is.

Martine set off blindly through the dripping trees ...

Blue lightning shuddered over the mountains ...

> **ACTIVITY**
>
> Discuss the **setting** of the story. What picture is in your mind of:
>
> a the weather?
>
> b the game reserve?

▶ **Character**

It is important that a reader feels that the **characters** are 'real'. They must be more than just a name.

We learn about Martine through what she **does** – **her actions.**

> **ACTIVITY**
>
> In this short extract from the story what **impression** do you get of Martine?
>
> Do you think she is brave / foolish / nervous / calm / curious / determined / frightened?
>
> Find evidence in the extract of what she does to support your view.

▶ **Detail**

In stories from **other cultures**, an important feature is the **detail** that many readers will find **unfamiliar**.

the setting   mangoes and gardenia blossoms

the animals   waterbuck   cobra   mamba

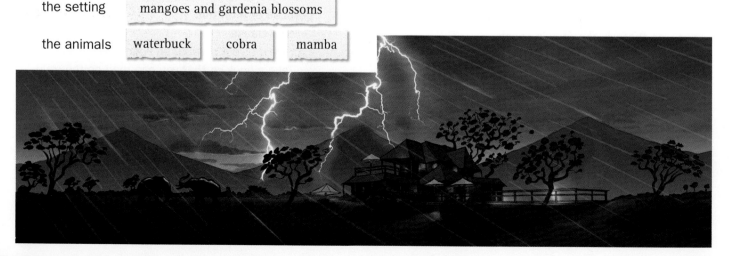

Writing together

> As a class, you are going to write a short extract from a story.
>
> The plot: Two characters are travelling on foot through either a busy city or the countryside.
>
> The setting: Somewhere you are familiar with.
>
> The characters: One character is brave and determined; the other is nervous and frightened.

Things to think about. Make notes.

The plot

- Where are the characters travelling?
- Why are they making the journey?

The setting

- How will you describe the setting?
- What details will you include that might be unfamiliar to some readers who do not live in your country?

  Think about:

  city   buildings / traffic / people's clothes / food

  countryside   plants / trees / weather / animals
- Is there anything really special in your country that could be part of the setting for your story?

Pyramids (Egypt)   Niagara Falls (Canada)   Uluru [Ayer's Rock] (Australia)

The characters

- Give your characters names.
- How will you help the reader understand the personality of the characters?
- Decide which character is brave and determined. What will this character do? How will this character behave on the journey?
- The other character is nervous and frightened. What will this character do? How will this character behave on the journey?

Write your story extract.

> **Remember!**
>
> Try to include details that are **familiar** for the part of the world you live in but might be **unfamiliar** to the reader. When we travel to different parts of the world we notice differences in:
>
> - food   • styles of buildings
> - clothes   • climate

WB p30

Conversation practice

1 Jack and Laura are talking. Look at the photos and the words in the box. What do you think they are talking about? How do you think they got the photos?

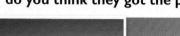

The Blue Mountains
New South Wales
vegetation
Uluru (Ayers Rock)
desert
aboriginal people
caves
rainforest
Queensland
National Park
The Great Barrier Reef
coral
scuba diving

2 🎧 1.11 Listen to Jack and Laura. Were you right?

3 🎧 1.11 Listen again. Try to spot two facts about each place. Make notes as you listen. Share your facts with the class.

4 Talk to your friends about the Australia photos. Try to remember as much detail as you can.

Start like this: *What do you think about these photos of Australia?*

Listening comprehension

1 🎧 1.12 Listen to Carrie. She is interviewing Professor Donovan from Brisbane University. What are the main areas that they talk about?

2 🎧 1.12 Read the following statements.
Listen again and write *T* (true) or *F* (false).

1 The Great Barrier Reef is one thousand kilometres long. _____
2 The Great Barrier Reef can be seen from space. _____
3 It is the only place in the world to have so many types of coral. _____
4 The Reef is a very rich wildlife habitat. _____
5 No endangered animals live on the Reef. _____
6 Because of global warming the sea temperature is rising. _____
7 Coral has died because the sea water is not warm enough. _____
8 The wildlife of the Reef will survive without the coral. _____
9 If the coral disappears, tourism will not be affected. _____
10 The only way to protect the Reef is to stop global warming. _____

healthy coral

bleached coral

Individual speaking

Choose a place of outstanding natural beauty or importance in your country and talk about it to the class.

WB p31 ▶

A great destination

4

Check-in

Spectacular buildings exist all over the world.
Some of them are modern, some are very ancient.
Some have a rich and interesting history.

*What is the most spectacular building you have
ever seen or visited?*
Did you like it? Why? / Why not?
*How could you find out about a building before you
visit it? List three methods.*

You are going to read some pages from a guidebook for
Thailand.

Reading

* The pages **explain and describe** the Grand Palace in
  Thailand's capital city.

  What is the capital of Thailand?

* The guidebook is written to **inform** visitors.
* It is also **written** to persuade.

  What does persuade mean?

* What do you think the guide persuades people to do?
* These words are on the pages you are going to read.

  destination   magnificence   decorate   ceremony
  remarkable   ignore   dazzling   royal   office

  What do they mean? Check in a dictionary.

Looking at language

* Dictionary: **adverbs**.
* Spelling: words ending **-ture** / **-sure**.

  Think of a word with each of these endings.

* Language development: **complex sentences**

Grammar

* Practise **reported statements and commands**.
* Practise **present simple for fixed future events**.
* Practise **phrasal verbs with *hang***.

Writing

* Learn about the **features of writing to
  inform / persuade**.
* Write a guide to the Grand Canyon.

  Where is the Grand Canyon?

* Write a guide to a local place you know.

Listening

* Holly and Ross's **conversation** about their schools.
* A **discussion** about two very different schools.

Speaking

* Talk in groups **about your school**.
* Tell the class about your school.

Guide to Thailand

Bangkok

The Grand Palace

Visitors from all around the world are truly amazed by the beauty and magnificence of the richly decorated buildings of the Grand Palace. "Stunning", "Dazzling", "Like a dream", "It's a must!" Comments like these appear repeatedly in online reviews written by visitors from every continent. The palace is one of the sights in Bangkok that every tourist should see. If you only have a little time in the city, make it your first destination.

Facts about the palace

The Grand Palace stands majestically on the east bank of the Chao Phraya river. It is a complex of many buildings and the whole site measures more than 218,400sq m. It is surrounded by a protective wall which is 1,900m long. There are three parts to the palace complex: the Outer Court, the Central Court and the Inner Court.

History

The Grand Palace was built by King Rama I in 1782. At first it was a group of traditional wooden buildings which the king used for his residence and his administration offices. More buildings have been added gradually over the centuries. The Grand Palace is no longer the permanent home of the kings of Thailand but many buildings are used for government offices, or for important occasions and ceremonies. The palace remains uniquely important to the people of Thailand.

Architecture

Golden towers and colourful, steep roofs rise impressively above the palace walls. Architectural styles include Thai, with other features from China, Cambodia and Europe. King Rama I encouraged Thai culture and literature. He told his architects to decorate his palace walls lavishly with scenes from the Thai story, the *Ramakien*.

These remarkable murals can be seen on some of the oldest buildings in the Outer Court of the palace.

Statues representing legendary creatures stand fiercely on guard at entrances and adorn façades, terraces and staircases.

Important buildings in the palace complex

This building in the Central Court was first a royal residence. Now it is used for royal ceremonies.

This building was a royal residence for nearly fifty years and foreign guests were received here. Now it is a great hall for state occasions.

This is one of the oldest buildings in the palace complex and is built in an ancient architectural style.

This building has eight towers, each one a different colour with its own special meaning.

There are many other buildings to see in the Outer Court and Central Court including libraries and galleries, with murals showing historic events and battles. In the past, the Inner Court was the residence of the queen, the royal children and their servants. It is not possible to visit this part of the palace.

The Grand Palace is open every day, 8.30–15.30.

Tips from International Visitors

Go by boat
"The river boat express stops a short walk away. You get a great view of the palace from the river."

Isabella, Argentina

Wear the right clothes
"Shorts and sleeveless tops are not allowed. If you don't have the right clothes, there is a place where you can hire them for your visit but it's better to have your own."

Shirin, Sri Lanka

Take …
"an umbrella. It will either pour with rain or the sun will burn you, so you'll need it whenever you go."

Kiera, UK

"plenty of water to drink. You'll be walking a lot and you'll get very hot."

Mai Ling, China

Ignore the tricksters
"They wait around for tourists and try to take them to some other place. They want your money! Walk on and don't stop."

David, Scotland

"A friendly man told us that the Grand Palace was closed. He said that he would take us to a palace that was open. He took us there, but afterwards he wanted us to buy expensive jewels from his friend's shop. Later, we found out that the jewels were fake and the Grand Palace wasn't closed at all!"

Dan, Canada

Don't forget
"Your ticket also admits you to the Vimanmek Mansion Museum which is near the Grand Palace. It's worth a visit."

Tracey, USA

1982 was the 200th year of Bangkok and the Mansion, built by King Rama V as a residence, was repaired. It is now a museum.

Reading comprehension

1 **Answer these questions.**

  1 What are some of the comments that people make about the palace?

  2 How big is the site of the palace?

  3 How long is the wall around it?

  4 Who built the palace?

  5 How many parts to the palace are there?

  6 What is the palace used for in the present time?

  7 Which architectural styles can you see in the buildings?

  8 How many important buildings of the palace complex are shown on the leaflet?

  9 Is it permitted to visit the Inner Court now?

  10 What sort of clothes can you not wear when you visit the palace?

2 **Number the sections of the text in the correct order.**
Write the section where you would look for the information below.

> Important buildings _____   Architecture _____   The Grand Palace _____
>   Tips _____   History _____   Facts _____

  1 the size of the palace complex _____

  2 who built the palace _____

  3 other buildings in the complex _____

  4 a plan of the palace complex _____

  5 things you should take when you visit _____

  6 how the palace walls are decorated _____

3 **Discuss your answers to these questions.**

  1 From what you can see in the guidebook, do you think the online review comments are right? Why? / Why not?

  2 Do you think the traditional eastern architectural style is attractive? Why? / Why not?

  3 Why do you think you have to wear the right clothes when you visit the palace?

  4 How would you make sure you did not get tricked by the tricksters?

4 **Write these adverbs next to their meanings.**

> *impressively   repeatedly   lavishly   uniquely   majestically*

  1 _____: in large quantity and expensively

  2 _____: in a way which makes people admire something or somebody

  3 _____: in a beautiful and grand way

  4 _____: in a special way

  5 _____: many times

Vocabulary check

Find these words in the text. Check any you are not sure of in a dictionary.

> magnificence   comment   continent   destination
> decorate   measure   residence   administration   office
> permanent   style   ceremony   literature   adorn
> façade   terrace   remarkable   murals   sleeveless
> hire   ignore   trickster   fake   dazzling   stunning   royal

Your views

● Would you be interested in visiting this palace? Why? / Why not?

● Which of the buildings shown in the guidebook do you think looks the most impressive?

● Which of the tips do you think is the most useful?

A Dictionary work
Adverbs derived from adjectives

- **Common adverbs** in a dictionary are set out like this.

> truly /'tru:li/ *adverb* completely

- More **unusual adverbs** come at the end of the **adjective** entry from which they are formed.

> majestic /mə'dʒestɪk/ *adjective* very beautiful or impressive **majestically** *adverb*

I **Find the adverbs in the guidebook that are formed from these adjectives.**

1 gradual 2 repeated 3 impressive

4 lavish 5 fierce

B Spelling
-ture and -sure endings

To decide whether a word ends in **-ture** or **-sure**, think about how the ending sounds.
- If it sounds /tʃ/ like *chair*, then the ending will be **-ture**.
  cul**ture** litera**ture**
- If it sounds /ʒ/ like *genre*, then the ending will be **-sure**.
  mea**sure** plea**sure**

The **-ture** ending is more common than the **-sure** ending.

I **Add -*ture* or -*sure* to complete the words in these sentences.**

1 I painted a pic_____ of my house.
2 The boy acted in a silly way.
  He was very imma_____.
3 I wrote my signa_____ at the bottom of the letter.
4 In my lei_____ time I like to go swimming.
5 It was a plea_____ to visit The Grand Palace.

C Language development
Simple and compound sentences

- You have learned about simple sentences.

I **How many main clauses are in this sentence?**

The Grand Palace was built by King Rama I in 1782.

- You have learned about writing **compound sentences** by joining one or more main clauses with conjunctions *and, but* or *or*.

2 **Underline the main clauses in this sentence.**

This building was a royal residence for nearly fifty years and foreign guests were received here.

Complex sentences

> Now learn about these.

- A **complex sentence** has a main clause and at least one subordinate clause.
- A **subordinate clause** has a verb but it does not make sense by itself.
- One example of a subordinate clause is a relative clause. It gives extra information about a part of the main clause.

3 **Read this example about the Grand Palace. Underline the main clause.**

At first it was a group of traditional buildings which the king used for his residence.

What information does the subordinate clause tell you?

- The sentence above could be written as two simple sentences.

At first it was a group of traditional buildings. The king used them for his residence.

- A complex sentence can contain more than one subordinate clause. It can contain more than one type of subordinate clause.
- A **participle clause** can begin with a present or past participle.

4 **Read this example from the guidebook. Underline the main clause. How many subordinate clauses are there?**

*There are many other buildings to see in the Outer Court and Central Court **including** libraries, and galleries with murals **showing** historic events and battles.*

5 **Discuss how the sentence above could be written as three sentences. Compare the complex sentence with the three simple sentences. Why do you think the guidebook uses a complex sentence?**

Grammar

1 Read.

A group of tourists was on a tour of the Grand Palace in Bangkok. One young man **thought** the palace **was** magnificent. His wife **said** that **she loved** the style of architecture. An elderly American tourist **said he would take** some photos of the statues. His wife **reminded him not to forget his** umbrella. One small boy **said he was** fed up. He **added that he was dying** of thirst and **asked his mother to give him** a drink. She **told him to stop** complaining! The tourist guide **asked** everyone to **follow her**. She **explained that there was** lots more to see.

The palace is magnificent.

I love the style of architecture.

I'll take some photos of the statues!

I'm fed up. I'm dying of thirst, too. Please, give me a drink, Mum.

Don't forget your umbrella, dear!

Stop complaining, Billy!

Follow me, please, everyone! There's lots more to see!

2 Answer these questions.

1 What did the young man and his wife think of the palace?
2 What did the elderly tourist say he would do?
3 Why was the small boy fed up?
4 What did his mother tell him to do?
5 What did the tourist guide ask everyone to do? Why?

Remember!
Reported statements
When the reporting verb is in the past tense (e.g. *said*), the verbs of the original direct speech usually change tense.
*"Lucy **is** tired," said John.* → *John said that Lucy **was** tired.*
When the reporting verb is the present tense (e.g. *says*), the verbs in the original direct speech do not change tense.
*"I **have attached** some photos."* → *Carrie says that she **has attached** some photos.*

3 Report the following statements, changing the tenses of the verbs.

1 "The Grand Palace is dazzling," said the tourists.
2 The guide told the visitors, "The statues represent legendary creatures."
3 "Visitors cannot enter the Inner Court," the guide explained.
4 She said, "Everyone has to wear suitable clothes."
5 "It will be an unforgettable visit," promised the guidebook.

Remember!
Reported commands
"Please, sit down!" said the teacher. → *The teacher **asked** the students **to sit down**.*
The teacher said, "Don't speak!" → *The teacher **told** the students **not to speak**.*

4 Report the following commands.

1 "Stop complaining, Billy!" said the woman.
2 "Please notice the remarkable murals, everyone," said the guide.
3 King Rama I ordered his architects, "Decorate the palace wall lavishly!"
4 "Please don't enter the Inner Court," the guide said to the tourists.
5 The guide said to her group, "Ignore the tricksters!"
6 "Don't believe what they say!" she told them.

Remember!
In reported speech pronouns and possessive adjectives can change, too.
I can't swim said George. → *George said that **he** couldn't swim.*

Always think of the meaning and you won't go wrong!

5 Complete these sentences. Report the direct speech and make any necessary changes.

1 "I'll help you." Jack told Laura that …
2 "Hand in your work, please." The teacher asked the class …
3 "The book isn't mine." The boy said that …
4 "We can't remember your name." The girls told me that …

42 Grammar: reported statements and commands

1 🎧 **1.14 Listen and read.**

Jack: Come on, Laura. Can't you walk a bit faster? Our bus **leaves** in two minutes.

Laura: Hang on a sec. That's my phone. I've got a text.

Jack: Don't read it now!

Laura: But it might be important. Oh! It's from Robert in Kenya.

Jack: Can't you read it on the bus?

Laura: He wants us to send him information about schools in the UK.

Jack: You can email him later.

Laura: Yes, and I can tell him about our school.

Jack: Good idea. Send him some photos, too.

Laura: He says he needs the information by the twenty-fifth. When**'s** the twenty-fifth?

Jack: It**'s** next Tuesday I think.

Laura: He says do we know there**'s** a solar eclipse in Nairobi next week.

Jack: He needs to tell the Science team about that, not us.

Laura: It's interesting though.

Jack: When **is** our next team meeting, by the way?

Laura: I think it**'s** on Saturday afternoon. I'll check when we get on the bus.

Jack: If we ever manage to catch the bus. Come on!

2 **Cover the dialogue and read the following statements. Write *T* (true) or *F* (false). Correct the false statements.**

1 Their bus leaves in ten minutes. _____
2 Laura gets a text from Robert in Kenya. _____
3 He needs some information by the twenty-fifth. _____
4 The twenty-fifth is next Wednesday. _____
5 There's a solar eclipse in Nairobi next month. _____
6 Jack thinks their next meeting is on Saturday. _____

3 **Ask and answer in pairs. Use the present simple of *to be*.**

1 What – day – tomorrow?
A: What day is it tomorrow? *B: It's …*
2 What – date – tomorrow?
3 What – date – next Saturday?
4 When – next exams?
5 When – next holiday?
6 When – next break?
7 What – next lesson?
8 What – programmes – TV – this evening?

4 **In pairs ask and answer using the present simple.**

9 am 3.30 pm 5.30 pm

Tuesday 4.45 pm 7.15 am

1 When – train – leave – tomorrow?
A: When does the train leave tomorrow?
B: It leaves at nine o'clock.
2 When – plane – land?
3 When – exams – start?
4 What time – film – begin?
5 What time – shops – shut – tomorrow?
6 When – taxi – get here?

Remember!
The **present simple** is used for fixed and certain events in the future.
- Statements about the calendar.
Today is Monday so tomorrow is Tuesday.
- Events which cannot change.
When is the next full moon?
- Planned, fixed events.
What time is the football match?
- With verbs such as *arrive, come, leave, start,* etc. when referring to plans, programmes or schedules.
Our train leaves in ten minutes.

Grammar extra p128

Writing

Features of writing to inform and persuade

> **The guidebook to the Grand Palace in Bangkok is non-fiction writing that gives the reader** information **and uses description to** persuade **people to visit.**

▶ **Tenses**

Both **past** and **present** tenses are used in the guide.

Past tenses are used for actions and descriptions that happened in the past.

ACTIVITY

Find three more examples of **past** and **present** tenses.

> The Grand Palace **was** built …

> He **told** his architects to decorate …

Present tenses are used for describing the Palace today and people's reactions.

> Visitors from all around the world **are** truly amazed …

> Golden towers and colourful, steep roofs **rise** impressively above the palace walls.

▶ **Information**

Visitors to the Grand Palace will want to know facts about it. The guide gives:

historical information

> built by King Rama I in 1782.

descriptive information

> It is surrounded by a protective wall which is 1,900m long.

practical information

> Shorts and sleeveless tops are not allowed.

ACTIVITY

Find one other **historical** fact, one other **descriptive** fact and one other piece of **practical** information.

▶ **Persuasive language**

The writer of the guidebook uses language designed to **persuade** people that the Palace is an interesting place to visit.

> … make it your first destination   NOT 'go if you can'   These remarkable murals …   NOT 'some wall pictures'

The guidebook also includes **positive opinions** from people who have seen the Palace.

> "Stunning"   "Dazzling"   "It's a must!"   "You get a great view of the palace from the river."

▶ **Layout**

The way the guidebook **looks** is very important. If the writer had just used text it would not look very interesting. There are different **presentational devices** to make the pages exciting and informative.

ACTIVITY

Find examples of these **presentational devices** and discuss them.

a sub-heading   b map   c plan

d photo   e caption   f tip box

Why do you think the writer has used them?

How do they make the pages more interesting?

Writing together

As a class, you are going to write about The Grand Canyon in North America. Below is a photograph, a map and a factfile.

You must include information, decide on the layout and think carefully about the language you use to persuade people to visit.

Read the fact file and look at the map and photograph.

Fact file:

One of the Seven Natural Wonders of the World

Location: north-west Arizona, North America

Size: app. 5,200sq km. / world's largest gorge / 1.6km at its deepest point / 29km at its widest point

Formation: took 3–6 million years to be formed by the Colorado River which on average is 300ft wide and 100ft deep

National Park: 1919

Population: Indian tribes – Hopi, Navajo, Havasupai and Paiute

Plants and animals: within the park – species of plants (1,500); birds (355); mammals (89); reptiles (47); amphibians (9); and fish (170)

Exploring the Grand Canyon
• on the ground – by foot / bike / mule / bus / jeep
• on the river – rafting
• in the air – small plane / helicopter

Nearly 5 million visitors each year

Opening times: South Rim – all year round / North Rim – from May to October (in winter months the North Rim is often blocked by snow)

Some persuasive language you could use:		
The views: unique	breathtaking	magnificent
The tours: informative	exciting	challenging
Add your own ideas.		

Write your guidebook page.

WB p39

Conversation practice

1 Ross and Holly are talking. Look at the pictures and the words in the box. What do you think they are talking about?

> facilities grounds technology sports hall stage
> science lab equipment canteen uniform

2 🎧 1.15 **Listen to Ross and Holly. Were you right?**

3 🎧 1.15 **Read the phrases in the box. Listen again and spot the phrases.**

> pretty big not really my thing Let's see … Well …
> out of this world I bet too good to be true

4 In groups talk about your school. List the facilities. How is your school different from Ross's school?

Start like this: *Do you think that we've got good facilities at our school?*

Listening comprehension

A

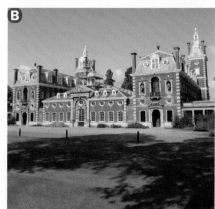

1 🎧 1.16 **Listen to Izzie and Dan. They are talking about their schools. Who goes to School A? Who goes to School B? Now answer the questions.**

1 Whose school has more students?
2 Whose school is older?
3 Which school has more sporting facilities?
4 What is a 'boarding school'?
5 How often does Dan see his family?
6 Whose school has bigger classes?
7 What does Izzie hate?
8 What does Dan dislike about his school?
9 What is a 'mixed school'?
10 What is the main difference between a state school and a private school?

B

Individual speaking

You are going to talk about your school.

`WB p40`

Beyond this world

Check-in

Every year scientists find out more about space. It is not essential to travel in space to find out about it, but some astronauts have travelled to the Moon to discover more.

> *How far away from Earth is the Moon?*
> *What is the force of gravity?*
> *How is the Moon different to Earth?*
> *Find out three other facts about the Moon.*

You are going to read a story about Kepler, a teenager who has lived all his life on the Moon.

Reading

- Stories about imaginary or future events in space are called **science fiction**.

> *What science fiction books or films do you know?*

- Some writers use **real scientific language**. Other writers invent **new ideas** and **new language**.

> *Do stories about space make science more interesting? Why? / Why not?*

- In the story, Kepler travels to Earth for the first time.

> *What would he find different when he arrived?*

- These words are in the story you are going to read.

> *groggy   exotically   sympathetic   feeble*
> *luxury   increase   brake*

> *What do they mean? Check in a dictionary.*

Looking at language

- Dictionary: **compound words**.
- Spelling: **y** sounding /ɪ/ and /aɪ/.
- Language development: **informal styles in fiction; prefix trans-**.

Grammar

- Practise **reported statements with tense shift**: past to past perfect, present perfect to past perfect.
- Practise quantifiers: *few, fewer, the fewest; little, less, the least*.
- Practise **phrasal verbs with take**.

> *List two phrasal verbs that use take.*

Writing

- Learn about the features of **science fiction writing**.
- Write the story of a boy's first visit to the Moon.
- Continue the science fiction story.

Listening

- Laura and Ross's **dialogue** about the performing arts.

> *List three different kinds of performance.*

- A tour guide's **commentary** on a London theatre.

Speaking

- Talk with a partner about **performance arts**.
- Tell the class about **a visit you made to a theatre or the cinema**.

Hello, Earth

Kepler Masterman is fifteen. He was the first child ever born on the Moon. He has been brought up with few luxuries because transport from Earth is expensive. His father is the Governor of the Moon and is travelling to Earth for important discussions. Kepler has travelled with his father by Moon-ferry to the space station where they transferred to an Earth-ferry. Now, they are approaching Earth and Kepler has his first close-up view of the world.

I craned my neck eagerly and looked through the port. I recognised the narrow spindle of central America, and then the steely shimmer of the Atlantic lay beneath us. It went on and on.
"The planet's all water!" I gasped.
"Seven tenths of it is," Father agreed.
"But … but. Oh, wow!" It was feeble, but what words could I have for it? A world that was seven tenths water! Why, on Moon, water was harder to get than oxygen, much harder. Breathing was free. You could breathe as deeply and as often as you wished. Now that the hydroponic gardens were going we didn't have to pay for our oxygen any more. But water was something else. Every ounce of it was worth its weight in Moon minerals. Dirt was removed by electrostatic filters in the labs and living units. Washing was a luxury and drinking a special delight.

There was no free water on Moon. Every ounce we used was extracted in the refinement of the ores we sent down to Earth. And the mining companies charged us for it – every drop! I had grown up thinking water was the most precious stuff in the Universe. Now with my own eyes I could see that Earth was covered with the stuff – slopping over with it.

We orbited across North Africa and Arabia. From my port I could see the island-spangled blueness of the Indian Ocean. Then the Pacific. I felt suddenly tired and a little sick. What sort of a place was this Earth and what were its people like? Half a world made of water, and yet they had charged us for every single cup. I shut my eyes and turned away from the port.
"You feeling groggy?" Father's voice was sympathetic. "They're starting their braking orbit and I guess you'll really notice the weight difference. Don't worry. It'll get worse before it gets better. But it will get better. Just hang on!"

To the Earth passengers from the space station I suppose the discomforts were minimal. Their apparent weight increased to double and momentarily three times their normal weight. I had not realised until this moment what my birthright of one-sixth Earth weight was going to mean when I tried to return 'home'. It was like a barrier separating me from all these other people. Already I weighed six times my normal weight. As the braking continued it increased to twelve times, to … the weight on my chest … I couldn't breathe. I felt as if my brain was going to burst.

When I came back to my senses the enormous pressure had lifted. I felt heavy and tired. I lifted my head and looked blurrily around. We had landed!

Kepler's father told him to lie still because he had had a nose-bleed. He asked a stewardess to help him. She explained to Kepler that the force of Earth's gravity had made his nose bleed. She got him an icepack and offered to get him a wheelchair if he couldn't walk.

"I'm going to be fine, thanks. It just takes a little practice, that's all."

"Of course. Perhaps you'd like to tidy up before you leave?"

I took her hint and plodded back down the aisle to the washroom. Good grief! I was a disaster area! I took off my jacket – how crudely cut it looked in comparison with the Earth fashions I'd seen on the ferry, and what rough material. Then I washed the rest of the blood off my face and combed my hair, what there was of it. It looked like a convict cut by Earth standards, but it would grow … I put on my jacket and plodded down to the exit hatch. I hesitated, my hand on the ramp rail, looking at the crowd of exotically dressed reporters, cameramen and casual bystanders milling around my father. It really was a new world down there at the end of the ramp.

from Goodbye to the Moon *by Monica Hughes*

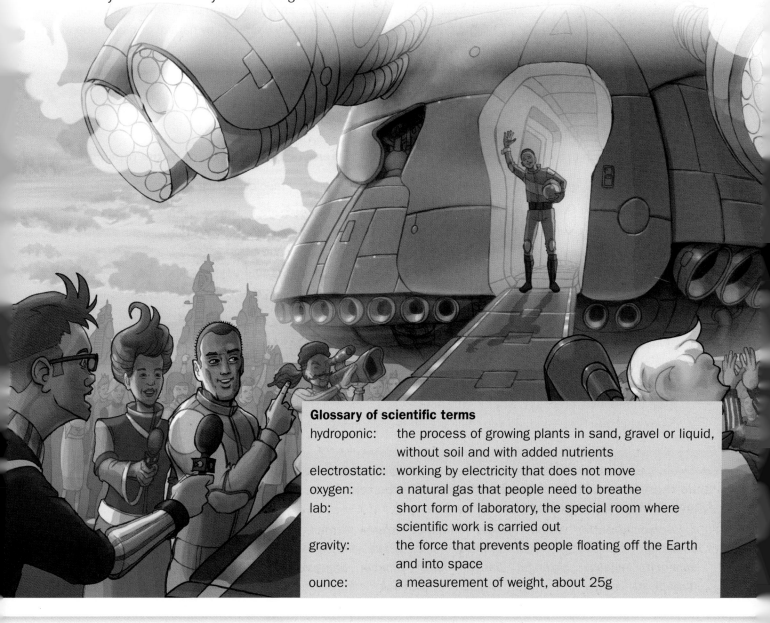

Glossary of scientific terms

hydroponic: the process of growing plants in sand, gravel or liquid, without soil and with added nutrients

electrostatic: working by electricity that does not move

oxygen: a natural gas that people need to breathe

lab: short form of laboratory, the special room where scientific work is carried out

gravity: the force that prevents people floating off the Earth and into space

ounce: a measurement of weight, about 25g

Reading comprehension

I Read these sentences. Write *T* (true) or *F* (false).

1 Seven tenths of the Earth is water. _____
2 The Atlantic Ocean looked blue and the Indian Ocean looked grey. _____
3 On the Moon, oxygen was more precious than water. _____
4 Kepler's weight on the Moon was one sixth of his weight on Earth. _____
5 The stewardess got Kepler an ice cream. _____
6 Kepler went to tidy up in the washroom. _____
7 He thought his hair was like a convict's. _____
8 His father was surrounded by reporters, cameramen and millers. _____

2 Match these phrases to their meanings then discuss the answers to the questions.

| island-spangled   good grief   worth its weight   disaster area   hang on |

a _____ of the same value in money as the value of the heaviness of something, often gold
b _____ covered with small, bright areas of land
c _____ wait for a short time, usually for something else to happen
d _____ an exclamation used when something is bad
e _____ land or a place that has been badly damaged by natural or man-made events

1 Why do you think Kepler calls himself 'a disaster area'?
2 A spangle is a bright shiny object used for decorating material and clothes. What does the phrase 'island-spangled' suggest that the ocean looks like?
3 Which two phrases do you think you would hear in informal conversation?
4 Who do you know who is worth his or her weight in gold?

3 Underline the adverbs. What part of speech are the other words? Match them to the meanings.

| groggy   steely   exotically   sympathetic   momentarily   crudely   feeble   casual   blurrily   eagerly |

1 in an attractively strange and unusual way
2 for a short time
3 done or made in a very simple way
4 without being able to see clearly
5 tired, weak and confused
6 hard, shiny and grey
7 not good enough to achieve the intended result
8 happening without being planned
9 able to understand someone's problems
10 with enthusiasm

4 Discuss your answers to these questions.

1 "What sort of a place was this Earth and what were its people like?" Why do you think Kepler asks himself this question?
2 Do you think the mining companies should have charged the people on the Moon for the water they saved from the refining process? Why? / Why not?
3 From what you have read, do you think life on the Moon was easier or more difficult than on Earth? Why?

Vocabulary check

Read these words. Find any you are unsure of in the text. Check them in a dictionary.

| governor   transfer   crane   spindle   shimmer   luxury   extract
refinement   ore   charge   stuff   Universe   slop   brake   discomfort
apparent   increase   birthright   barrier   burst   minimal   pressure
nose-bleed   stewardess   force   icepack   wheelchair   comparison
convict   hatch   hesitate   ramp   rail   bystander   mill   around |

Your views

● If you were going to live on the Moon would you be excited or horrified? Why?
● Do you think Kepler is a person who enjoys new experiences? Explain your answer.
● Do you think Kepler will seem strange to people on Earth? Why? / Why not?

A Dictionary work
Compound words

- **Compound words** are two or more words used as a single word. They are shown as separate entries in a dictionary.

over /ˈəʊvə/ *adjective, adverb, preposition* in a higher position

overall /ˌəʊvərˈɔːl/ *adverb* when everything is considered

overcoat /ˈəʊvəˌkəʊt/ *noun* [C] a long warm coat

overcome /ˌəʊvəˈkʌm/ *verb* [T] to succeed in dealing with a problem (**overcomes, overcoming, overcame**)

overdue /ˌəʊvəˈdjuː/ *adjective* if something is overdue, it should have been done before now

1 Find these compound words beginning with *post-*.
1 someone whose job it is to collect and deliver post
2 message that is added to the end of a letter
3 the study done after a university degree
4 a medical examination of a body to find the cause of death

B Spelling
y sounding /ɪ/ and /aɪ/

- In some words, **y** has the short sound of /ɪ/ as in *hill*.
  …*water was harder to get than* **oxygen**…
  Father's voice was very **sympathetic**.
- In some words, **y** has the sound /aɪ/ as in *high*.
  Now that the **hydroponic** *gardens were going* …
  … *casual* **bystanders** *milling around my father* …

1 Add *i* or *y* to complete each word.
1 h__drogen   2 n__lon
3 st__le   4 rh__thm

2 Match each word in the box to the correct definition.

cymbal python gymnasium lyrics

1 the words of a song
2 a large snake that kills animals by wrapping itself around them
3 a musical instrument that is a thin, circular piece of metal
4 a room or club with equipment for doing physical exercise

C Language development
Informal styles in fiction:
Missing words

- In informal conversation, speakers sometimes leave out words. *"You feeling groggy?"*

1 Which word is missing from the sentence?

- It can be shortened to *"Feeling groggy?"*
- Very informally, the enquiry may be reduced to the adjective alone: *"Groggy?"*

Sentences beginning with conjunctions

- In formal writing, it is best to avoid beginning a sentence with conjunctions *and, but* and *or*.
- In fiction, dialogue sentences beginning with *But, And* and other conjunctions appear often, especially in conversation.
  "But it will get better."

2 Find sentences in the reading text beginning with *But* and *And*. Join each sentence with the one before it in the text. Use the conjunction in the formal way. Compare them with the text. Why do you think the writer divided the sentences?

Sentences without a main clause

- In formal writing, a sentence must have a main clause with a complete verb. In the story, Kepler is expressing his thoughts. Some short sentences do not contain a main clause with a complete verb.
  Then the Pacific.
- Exclamations do not need to contain a main clause.
  A world that was seven tenths water!

3 Why do you think the writer uses short sentences in this way?

Word building: prefix *trans-*

- The prefix *trans-* comes from Greek and means *across*.
  At the space station, they **transferred** *to an Earth ferry.*
- A **transatlantic** flight is one which flies across the Atlantic Ocean.

4 Complete these words. What do they mean?

_____port   _____parent

Grammar

1 Read.

At last the journey was over. Kepler felt heavy and tired. His father told him not to worry and explained that they **had landed** safely. He told Kepler to lie still. He said he **had had** a nose-bleed and **had lost** quite a lot of blood. The stewardess explained that the force of gravity **had made** his nose bleed.

The reporters who were waiting when the Earth-ferry arrived wanted to interview Kepler. He told them he **had been** very excited about coming to Earth for the first time and said that the views of Earth from space **had been** incredible. He told them that mostly he **had enjoyed** the journey but that he **had felt** frightened towards the end because he could not breathe.

We've landed.

You've had a nose-bleed.

You've lost quite a lot of blood.

The force of gravity made your nose bleed.

I was excited about coming to Earth.

I felt frightened towards the end.

The views of Earth from space were incredible.

Mostly I enjoyed the journey.

2 Cover the text and say if the following sentences are true or false. Check your answers. Correct the false statements.

1 Kepler felt tired at the end of the journey.
2 His father said he had had a serious accident.
3 His nose had bled because of the force of gravity.
4 Kepler told the reporters that he had not wanted to come to Earth.
5 He said that the views of Earth from space had been incredible.
6 He said that he had not enjoyed the journey.

3 Report the direct speech.

1 "You have lost a lot of blood," said Kepler's father.
   Kepler's father said that he had lost a lot of blood.
2 "I have never felt worse," Kepler said.
3 Kepler told his father, "I've washed the blood off my face."
4 "We've had an amazing journey," Kepler told the reporters.
5 "I slept for part of the journey," he said.
6 He said, "We saw the most amazing views of Earth."
7 "The force of gravity made your nose bleed," explained the stewardess.
8 "I was happy to help you," she added.

4 Work in pairs. Report the speech bubbles. Choose from the reporting verbs in the box.

explained   shouted   whispered   promised
admitted   complained

I AM VERY ANGRY!

I broke the vase.

The books are mine.

Shh! The baby is sleeping.

Someone has taken my pen.

I'll help you, Mum.

Remember!
Reported statements
When the **reporting verb** is in the past tense (e.g. said), the verbs of the original direct speech change.
*"I **have lost** my purse," said Lucy.* →
*Lucy said that she **had lost** her purse.*
*Joe said, "I **broke** the window, Sue."* →
*Joe told Sue that he **had broken** the window.*

1 🎧 [1.18] Listen and read.

Holly: I had an email from Tippi in Thailand yesterday.

Jack: Really? What did she say?

Holly: She's doing a web page about the theatre in different countries. She asked me to send her some information about the theatre in the UK.

Ross: I'll help if you like. I know a bit about the Globe Theatre in London.

Holly: OK. Thanks. Tippi said that Usha had sent her lots of emails about the theatre in India but she's had **fewer** replies from the other teams.

Ross: I've had no emails or messages at all this week.

Jack: I've had two. That's **the fewest** since we started the project.

Ross: I'm sure Sergei could help Usha. The theatre's very important in Russia, I think.

Holly: Yes, and ballet, too. Which reminds me … She sent **a few** photos of Thai dancers. They're amazing! … Well, you could show **a little** enthusiasm!

Ross: Sorry, but I don't have **the least** interest in Thai dancing.

Jack: And I have even **less**!

Holly: Honestly! You're terrible!

Ross: Only joking! Let's see the photos.

Jack: Wow! Look at those masks and gold headdresses. They're amazing!

Holly: Told you so!

2 Answer these questions.

1 Why did Tippi email Holly?

2 Why could Sergei help Tippi?

3 At first, do Ross and Jack show a lot of interest in the photos from Tippi?

4 Are they serious or pretending? How do you know?

3 Work in pairs. Make phrases with either *a little* or *a few* and the words below. Then make sentences using the phrases.

1 money   2 food   3 children   4 time

5 emails   6 heat   7 messages   8 success

4 Complete these sentences with *little, a little, few* or *a few*.

1 I'm afraid I can give you _____ information about the exams.

2 Unfortunately there are _____ students studying Art.

3 Peter showed _____ interest in the work at first but soon grew bored.

4 I've got _____ minutes to spare. Shall I help you?

5 Work in pairs. Make sentences using *fewer … than* or *less … than*.

1 Cairo – Paris – inhabitants

   I think Paris has fewer inhabitants than Cairo.

2 Thailand – England – sunshine

3 India – England – cold weather

4 a rainforest – a desert – wildlife

6 Complete these sentences with *the fewest* or *the least*.

1 Which class has _____ students?

2 Jack does not have _____ interest in ballet.

3 Of all the players Simon scored _____ goals.

4 Which man earns _____ money?

> **Remember!**
> We use **few**, **fewer** and **the fewest** with countable nouns.
> *There are **few** students studying Chinese.*
> *Ann studies **fewer** subjects than her brother.*
> *Our team scored **the fewest** points in the quiz.*
> We use **little**, **less** and **the least** with uncountable and abstract nouns.
> *John shows **little** interest in going to university.*
> *Meg spends **less** money than her sister.*
> *July is often the month with **the least** rain.*
>
> **few** = not many   **a few** = some
> **little** = not much   **a little** = some

Grammar extra p128 ▸

Features of science fiction writing

> **Writing stories about what may happen in the future is called** science fiction.
> **The author of** *Goodbye to the Moon* **has imagined a future where people have been living on the Moon for so many years that children have been born there.**

▶ **Tenses**

Like all stories, science fiction is usually written in **past tenses**.

I **craned** my neck eagerly …   Father's voice **was** sympathetic.

ACTIVITY
Find three more examples of **past tenses**.

▶ **First person**

If the author decides to be a character in the story, it is written in the **first person**.

I had grown up thinking that water was the most precious stuff in the Universe.

We orbited across North Africa and Arabia.

ACTIVITY
Find three more examples of the **first person**.

▶ **Setting**

Science fiction stories are either set on the Earth far into the future, or in other worlds. Because the **setting** is imaginary, the writer must help readers to 'see' where the story is taking place and what conditions are like.

On the Moon: There was no water on the Moon.   Washing was a luxury and drinking a special delight.

In the spaceship: … you'll really notice the weight difference.   I couldn't breathe. I felt as if my brain was going to burst.

ACTIVITY
Discuss what **impression** you get of:
• life on the Moon
• travelling in the spaceship.

▶ **Technical / scientific language**

Science fiction writers use the **language of science and technology** from the real world as far as they can.

Now that the **hydroponic** gardens were going …   Dirt was removed by **electrostatic** filters …

You will find that in some science fiction stories authors make up words because they are describing gadgets that only exist in their imagination!

Writing together

On Kepler's return journey to the Moon, his cousin Conrad goes with him. Conrad was born on Earth and has never visited the Moon. They have taken the Earth-ferry to the space station, and they are now on the Moon-ferry approaching the Moon.

As a class, you are going to write a science fiction extract about Conrad's first impressions of the Moon as he looked through the porthole.

Things to think about.

You must imagine that you are Conrad and write in the **first person**.

Begin by explaining where you were and where you were going. **Use past tenses**.

Let the reader know how you felt about what was happening. Were you excited / bored / frightened / worried?

Imagine that you looked through the porthole and saw the landscape in the photograph.

Study the photograph carefully. Make notes on what you see and how you would **describe** it.

Some useful vocabulary

vast   deserted   dusty   lifeless   eerie   desolate   grey   still   colourless

When Kepler came to Earth he suffered from the weight difference. He was six times heavier than on the Moon due to gravity. He had a nose-bleed and felt 'heavy and tired'.

You experienced being six times lighter as you landed on the Moon. **Describe** how you felt. Was it a horrible sensation? Was it an amazing experience?

- **Write your story extract.**

  Remember!
  - Write in **past tenses**.
  - Use the **first person** – this has happened to you.
  - Describe what you saw – **the setting** – in detail.

WB p50

Conversation practice

1 Ross and Laura are talking. Look at the pictures and the words in the box. What do you think they are talking about?

> play   comedy   hilarious   ballet   graceful   thriller
> action films   fast-moving   special effects   classical music
> orchestra   pop   rock   bands   CDs

2 Listen to Ross and Laura. Were you right?

3 Read the phrases in the box. Listen again and spot the phrases.

> a couple of   Actually   not my thing   though   How about   really into

4 In groups talk about the arts like Ross and Laura.
Start like this: *Have you ever been to the theatre?*

Listening comprehension

1 A group of visitors is enjoying a tour of the Globe Theatre in London. Listen to their guide.

2 Read these sentences. Listen again and write *T* (true) or *F* (false) for each sentence.

1 In the 16th century few people enjoyed the theatre. ___
2 The Globe was the only theatre on the bank of the Thames. ___
3 The original Globe Theatre burnt down. ___
4 In Shakespeare's day rich people stood to watch the plays. ___
5 Some people sat on comfortable, wooden seats. ___
6 'The pit' is another name for the stage. ___
7 The new Globe is totally different from the original theatre. ___
8 The theatre is round in shape. ___
9 The theatre is made of wood and steel. ___
10 Music for the plays is provided by CDs. ___
11 A roof covers part of the theatre. ___
12 Audiences are much bigger today than they were in Shakespeare's time. ___

Individual speaking

Talk about a visit to the theatre or to the cinema.

WB p51

I remember

Touching the Void
Joe Simpson

Check-in

We learn about the lives of famous people through biographies and autobiographies. Sometimes the lives of ordinary people can be just as interesting.

What is the difference between a biography and an autobiography?
What famous people from the past have you learned about by reading about their lives?
Do you know of an autobiography of someone alive now who you like or admire?

You are going to read an extract from an autobiography that recalls an episode when the author was a teenager.

Reading

- The author grew up in Delhi, India. The Himalayas are also mentioned.

Find India, Delhi and the Himalayas on a world map.

- In the extract, the author **recounts** the stress of the exam period.

Do you think the exam period is stressful? Why? / Why not?

- These words are in the extract you are going to read.

  suffer   exhausted   pure   wily
  tease   fling   suspend

What do they mean? Check in a dictionary.

Looking at language

- Dictionary: **derived words**.
- Spelling: **silent t**.
- Language development: **subordinate clauses**.

What is a clause?

Grammar

- Practise **time clauses using all tenses** with *when, after, while, before, until, as soon as*.
- Practise **language of agreement**.
- Practise **phrasal verbs with** *do*.

Writing

- Learn about the features of **autobiographical writing**.
- Write about an autobiographical event from notes.
- Write about a true autobiographical incident.

Listening

- Jack and Holly's **discussion** about schoolwork and hobbies.
- Laura's **conversation** with her parents about schoolwork and the website project.

How often do you discuss your schoolwork with your parents?

Speaking

- Talk with a partner about **your schoolwork and your hobbies**.
- Tell the class about your hobbies and the balance with your schoolwork.

How many hobbies or interests outside schoolwork do you have?

THE HONEY-SELLER

Climbing the Mango Trees is the autobiography of Madhur Jaffrey, a well-known writer who was born and brought up in India. The autobiography tells of the author's childhood in Delhi, the capital city. This episode recounts the preparation for exams and a visit from a memorable salesman who came to the house one day during the study period.

As soon as I got home from school, hot and sweaty from cycling, my mother would produce cold phirini from the refrigerator. This was a very light, cardamom-scented pudding made with coarsely ground rice that my mother set in shallow terracotta bowls. I would slide the spoon in and begin eating. The sweet, cool, milky pudding, tasting of the cardamom and pistachios with an earthy aroma of terracotta, went down smoothly …

There was no time to rest afterwards. May was the time for our annual exams and all of April had to be spent doing revision … While I studied in my hot back room, my mother sat knitting for my sisters in their frigid Himalayan convent. In the superheated Delhi of April, I could hardly even look at wool, let alone touch it. My mother just carried on heroically. Each examination was three hours long … On most days there were two exams with a break for lunch. Before I left early in the morning, armed with sharpened pencils, pens freshly filled with ink, ink bottles, rulers and erasers, my mother would appear with a plate containing two almond balls. My mother firmly believed that almonds were brain food and that any child sent off to write two examination papers for six hours unfortified with almond balls was surely suffering from the grossest form of neglect … I would return home, ink-stained and exhausted, and immediately begin studying for the next day's exams. My mother never asked me how I had fared. She always assumed I would do well.

Often she would try and distract me from my studies if she thought I was working too hard. One afternoon, when the servants were off-duty, she called me saying, "Come, come, there is a man here selling honey." By the time I came out, the man was well into his sales pitch … "Purer honey than this you can never hope to find. Look at its fine golden colour. See, see it still has pieces of honey-comb suspended in the middle. Smell it. The odour of nature's flowers …" My mother cut right to the chase, "But how do I know it is pure? What proof do you have?" She was hoping she had stumped him.

He turned out to be wilier than that. "What proof, you want to know? The oldest proof in the world. It has worked since the beginning of time. First you catch a fly and then you throw it into the honey. It will sink. If the honey is impure, it will keep sinking and die. If the honey is pure, it will rise to the surface and fly away." At that, he swung his hand in the air and caught a fly, flinging it immediately into the honey. It sank. Then it started to rise, higher and higher until it reached the surface and flew away. My mother was so impressed, she bought several jars and I went back to my studies.

That evening, when the cook returned from his afternoon break and my mother recounted the honey story, he said, "Arey memsa'ab [Oh, lady] you have been completely duped. I can do exactly same thing with sugar syrup." Our cook seemed as adept at catching flies with his hand as the honey man. He caught one and threw it into a jar of sugar syrup that my mother kept for sweetening our fresh lime juice. The fly sank, then rose to the top and flew away. We teased our mother mercilessly.

from Climbing the Mango Trees
by Madhur Jaffrey

Glossary

cardamom: a spice for giving a scented taste to food
pistachio: a kind of nut
terracotta: baked clay
convent: a type of school for girls
almond: a kind of nut

1   Answer these questions.

1   What part of the author's life does this autobiography cover?
2   What were the ingredients of the pudding that was produced from the refrigerator?
3   In what part of India were Madhur's sisters at school?
4   What was Madhur's mother doing for her daughters in the Himalayas?
5   How many exams did Madhur have on most days?
6   What things did she take with her?
7   What was in the balls that Madhur's mother gave her before she left for her exams?
8   What was the man selling?
9   Why did Madhur's mother buy several jars of honey?
10   Where did the cook throw the fly and what did it do?

2   Find these phrases. Match them to the meanings then discuss the questions.

    off-duty
    armed with
    sales pitch
    cut to the chase

1   to go straight to the main point
2   an enthusiastic description of a product intended to make someone want to buy it
3   having free time and not required to carry out any work or tasks
4   having one or more weapons for carrying out an attack or fighting in a battle

Why do you think the writer says she was 'armed with' pencils, pens, ink and erasers?
One of these phrases comes from film-making in Hollywood, USA. Can you guess which?

3   Discuss your answers to these questions.

1   What was the weather like in Delhi and in the Himalayas in April? How do you know?
2   What sort of person do you think Madhur's mother was? Explain your answer.
3   Why did Madhur and her family tease their mother after the incident with the honey?
4   Do you think the honey-seller tricked Madhur's mother or was he just a good salesman?
5   Madhur Jaffrey is well-known for writing a particular kind of book. From details she mentions in the text, can you guess what kind of books she wrote?

Vocabulary check

List the three parts of speech in this group of words. List the words next to the correct part of speech.

sweaty	coarsely	shallow	annual	knit	frigid	unfortified	suffer	gross	exhausted	fare
assume	distract	pure	suspend	stump	wily	sink	fling	dupe	adept	tease	mercilessly

_____   _____

                _____

_____   _____

                _____

_____   _____

                _____

Helpful hint! Find each word in the text. Read the sentence to help you decide what part of speech it is. If you're not sure of the meaning, look it up.

Your views

● Think of three different kinds of food or drink that you remember from when you were younger. Why do you remember them particularly?
● Does it help to have a distraction from studying during the exam period? Why? / Why not?
● Do you think Madhur was a good student? How do you know? Find at least two reasons.

Looking at language

A Dictionary work
Derived words

- In Unit 4, we looked at adverbs **derived** from adjectives, and how more unusual adverbs appear at the end of the adjective entry.

> **coarse** /kɔːs/ *adjective* not smooth or soft; consisting of rough or thick pieces – **coarsely** *adv*.

- Dictionaries sometimes give other types of **derived** words in the form of Word Family boxes.

> **pure** /pjʊə/ *adjective* a pure substance has nothing mixed with it that might spoil its quality
> Word family: **pure**
> - purely *adv*   - purist *n*
> - purify *vb*   - impure *adj*
> - purity *n*   - impurity *n*

- The words in the family will also appear as entries to give you more information and, sometimes, more **derived** words.

> **purify** /ˈpjʊərɪfaɪ/ (**purifies**, **purifying**, **purified**) *verb* [T] to make clean by removing dirt or other harmful substances

I   **Look up these words in a dictionary.
Find the members of each word family.**

1 believe   a 3 nouns   b 1 verb
            c 2 adjectives   d 1 adverb
2 produce   a 5 nouns   b 1 verb
            c 3 adjectives   d 1 adverb

B Spelling
Silent t

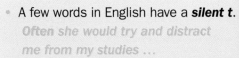

- A few words in English have a **silent t**.
  *Often she would try and distract
  me from my studies …*
- There are not that many of these words, but you need to learn them.

I   **Like *often*, some words have a *silent t* before the *en* ending.**

1 lis**t**en
Write: a the word meaning *one who listens*
         b the past tense of *I listen*
2 fas**t**en
Write: a the opposite of *to fasten*
         b the present tense of *I was fastening*

C Language development
More about subordinate clauses

- In Unit 4, you learned that a **complex sentence** has a main clause and at least one **subordinate clause**. You looked at complex sentences with
  - a main clause + a **relative clause**.
  - a main clause + an *-ing* **participle clause**.
- You also saw that a sentence can contain more than one subordinate clause.
- There are several types of subordinate clauses. These clauses add different information into the sentence.

I   **Read about the types of subordinate clause and examples from the extract.**

- **-ed participle clause**   *I would return home, ink-stained and exhausted*
- **that clauses**   *My mother firmly believed that almonds were brain food*
- **time clauses**   *While I studied in my hot back room, my mother sat knitting for my sisters*

> Sometimes a writer uses several subordinate clauses. A sentence can end up being quite long.
> *My mother firmly believed that almonds were brain food and that any child sent off to write two examination papers for six hours unfortified with almond balls was surely suffering from the grossest form of neglect.*

2   **The example sentence above is made up of several clauses. Find the main clause, two *that* clauses and one *-ed* participle clause.**

> *Look for the clauses in a long sentence to help you understand it.*

Word building: suffix: -hood

> The autobiography tells of the author's **childhood**.
> The suffix *-hood* can be added to family words to express:
> - the state of being a parent: *motherhood, fatherhood*
> - the relations between people: *brotherhood, sisterhood*
> - different times in a person's life: *childhood, boyhood, girlhood, adulthood*
> There are a few other words with this suffix, e.g. *falsehood, likelihood, neighbourhood.*

3   **Guess the meanings, then check in a dictionary.**

Grammar

1 Read.

It was the time of exams. **As soon as** Madhur got home from school, hot and tired, her mother produced a sweet rice pudding for her to eat. **After** she had eaten the pudding, there was no time to rest. She went to her room to continue revising. **While** Madhur studied in her room, her mother sat knitting on the terrace. **Before** Madhur left for school every day, her mother gave her two almond balls to eat. She was not happy **until** Madhur had eaten them both. Almond balls were brain food!

One afternoon **while** Madhur was studying, a honey-seller came to the house. He persuaded them that his honey was pure and Madhur's mother bought several jars. **When** she told the cook about the honey-seller and what he had done, the cook laughed. "I can do the same thing with sugar syrup," he said. "**When** I throw a fly into the syrup, it will rise to the top and fly away." And he was right! Madhur's mother had been duped!

2 Answer these questions.

1 What did Madhur's mother give her as soon as she got home from school?
2 What did she do after she had eaten the pudding?
3 What did Madhur do while her mother sat knitting?
4 What happened while Madhur was studying one afternoon?

3 Remember!

Time clauses: talking about the present
Time clauses are used for actions which happen regularly.
I always have breakfast before I leave for school.
We don't go into school until the bell rings.
(… has rung.)

Finish these sentences. Use present tenses.

1 As soon as I get home, I always …
2 Before I have dinner, …
3 When I have finished eating, …

4 Remember!

Time clauses: talking about the future
Future tense / Imperative tense in the main clause; present tense in the time clause.
When Sam leaves school, he will go to university.
He won't have any money until he finds a job.
(… has found a job.)
Take off your shoes before you come in!

Use your own ideas to finish these sentences.

1 I'll send you a postcard when …
2 Lucy won't be happy until …
3 Please send me a text as soon as …

5 Remember!

Time clauses: talking about the past
- Regular actions in the past.
  While Madhur studied, her mother sat knitting.
- Two actions happening at the same time.
  Yesterday while Ann was sleeping, her mother was preparing a surprise.
- A long action interrupted by a sudden action.
  While Madhur was studying, a honey-seller came to the house.
- One action finishes before another happens.
  After they had eaten they slept.
- One action is quickly followed by another.
  When she told the cook the story, he laughed.
  As soon as she got home, she had something to eat.
  She ate the almond cakes before she left for school.

Think of your own examples of the five forms. Use these conjunctions.

when   after   while   as soon as   before   until

1 🎧 1.22 Listen and read.

Ross: What's the matter, Laura? You look really fed up.

Laura: I am fed up. I've had a terrible row with Mum and Dad.

Holly: So what? I'm always arguing with my parents.

Ross: **So am I!**

Laura: But this is serious. They want me to stop working on the project.

Ross: You're joking. I don't believe it.

Holly: **Neither do I!** You can't leave the project, Laura!

Laura: They say I'm spending too much time on the project and neglecting my school work.

Jack: And are you?

Laura: I don't think so. My marks have been OK this term.

Ross: **So have mine** and I've spent hours and hours on the project.

Laura: I tried to persuade them but I couldn't.

Jack: **Nor could I.** I tried talking to them, too.

Holly: This is a disaster! We need you, Laura!

Ross: Absolutely! You're our computer expert. We can't do without you.

Laura: Well, I'll try talking to them again.

Jack: And **so will I** but I don't hold out much hope.

2 Cover the dialogue and say if the following sentences are true or false. Check your answers. Correct the false statements.

1 Laura is feeling happy today.
2 She has had a row with her brother.
3 Her parents want her to stop working on the project.
4 Laura says that she has been neglecting her school work.
5 Laura is an essential member of the team.
6 Jack thinks his parents will change their minds.

3 Agree with Ross.

1 "I'm hungry."
   So am I.
2 "I like the summer holidays."
3 "I've worked hard this term."
4 "I must pass my exams."
5 "I'll revise for the next test."
6 "I watched TV yesterday."
7 "I can use a computer."
8 "I'm feeling good today."

4 Agree with Holly.

1 "I don't like cold weather."
   Neither do I. Or: Nor do I.

2 "I can't speak Chinese."
3 "I've never been to Japan."
4 "I wasn't late for school today."
5 "I didn't enjoy my last exam."
6 "I shouldn't eat too many sweets."

5 Work in pairs. Agree with these statements. Use the words in brackets.

1 Jane failed her driving test. (her brother)
   So did her brother.
2 The boys love holidays. (their parents)
3 We didn't enjoy that film. (we)
4 Jack never arrives late. (Laura)
5 Ben's going to New York. (Martin)
6 John won't eat meat. (his sister)
7 An ostrich can't fly. (a penguin)
8 Laura's bought a new dress. (Holly)

Remember!
Agreeing with affirmative statements:
A: I am hungry. B: So am I.
A: I like sport. B: So do I.
Agreeing with negative statements:
*A: Joe **didn't** sleep. B: Nor **did** we. / Neither **did** Bill.*
*A: They **won't** help. B Neither **will** Sue. / Nor **will** I.*

Grammar extra p128 ▶

Writing

Features of autobiography

> An **autobiography** is a book someone writes about his or her own life.
> It is written in the first person and the writer recounts facts, experiences and feelings.

▶ **First person**

Autobiographies are written in the **first person**.

> As soon as **I** got home from school …

> **We** teased our mother mercilessly.

ACTIVITY
Find three more examples of the **first person** in the extract.

▶ **Past tenses**

People writing autobiographies are recounting what has happened to them.
They write in **past tenses**.

> My mother firmly **believed** …

> Each examination **was** three hours long …

ACTIVITY
Find three more examples of **past tenses** in the extract.

▶ **Factual information**

An autobiography gives the reader **facts** about the person's life.

> There was no time to rest afterwards.

> … I studied in my hot back room …

ACTIVITY
Find three more examples of **facts** in the extract.

▶ **Precise details**

The writer of an autobiography wants readers to have a clear, vivid picture of what his/her life
was like. It is important that the writer includes **precise details**.
Madhur Jaffrey does not write: 'When I got home from school, mother gave me some food. It was nice.'

She uses adjectives and adverbs to create a vivid picture.

She was: **hot** and **sweaty** from cycling …

She was given: **cold phirini**

That was: **a very light, cardamom-scented pudding** made with **coarsely ground rice** …

She enjoyed it: The **sweet, cool, milky pudding** … went down **smoothly**.

ACTIVITY
Find **detailed writing** in the extract about:
* the weather
* the examinations
* the honey

▶ **Thoughts and feelings**

An autobiography would be quite boring if it were just a list of facts. The reader wants to know how the writer **felt** and what he/she **thought**.

> … I could hardly even look at wool, never mind touch it.

> … I would return home, ink-stained and exhusted …

What did Madhur's mother **think** about:
a how her daughter would do in the exams?
b the trick the honey-seller showed her?

Writing together

> **As a class, you are going to write a short** autobiography **from the notes below. The notes give you the** facts **about an incident in this person's life. You must think carefully about his** thoughts and feelings.

Read the facts **about an incident in Jack's life.**

Jack remembers when he was 13 years old and he was picked as a member of the school swimming team. His school was competing against five other schools for the swimming trophy. Jack was swimming backstroke. The others in his team all won their races. If Jack won his race, his school would win the trophy. He swam two lengths of the pool. After one length he was in third position. He swam the second length much quicker and came first.

Things to think about.

Before the competition
* What did your teacher say to the group before the competition began?
* How did you feel?
* Did you think your team had a chance of winning the trophy or not? Why?

The other races
* One of your team won his race easily. How did you feel?
* One of your team only just managed to win. How did you feel?

Your race
* You knew if you won your race, your school would win the trophy.
* How did you feel standing on the edge of the pool waiting for the race to begin?
* What were you thinking / feeling as you swam the first length?
* What were you thinking / feeling when you were behind two other swimmers after the first length?
* What did you say to yourself as you swam the second length?
* How did you feel when you came first?

> *You have to imagine you are Jack.*

Write the autobiography.

> **Remember!**
> * Write in the **first person** and the **past tense**.
> * Include the **factual information** about the team, the competition, etc.
> * Include lots of **precise detail** so the reader can clearly imagine the event.
> * Most importantly – let the reader know your **thoughts and feelings**.

WB p59

Conversation practice

I **Jack and Holly are talking. Look at the pictures and the words in the boxes. What do you think they are talking about?**

homework compositions presentations reading studying learn by heart revising tests exams private lessons	English maths science French history geography music art PE IT

2 🎧 **Listen to Jack and Holly. Were you right?**

3 🎧 **Listen again. Who works harder, Jack or Holly?**

4 **How well do you balance your schoolwork and your hobbies? Talk in groups.**
Start like this: *How much time do you spend on your schoolwork?*

Listening comprehension

I 🎧 **Laura is talking to her mum and dad. Listen to the conversation.**

2 🎧 **Read these questions. Listen again and answer.**

1 What do Laura's parents want her to give up?
2 According to them, what is she spending too little time on?
3 What does she do as soon as she gets home from school?
4 How does Laura defend the project?
5 What do her parents want her to be?
6 What does Laura want as a profession?
7 Do her parents approve of this?
8 Who says what? Laura? Her mother? Her father? Write *L, M* or *F.*

a "You're starting to neglect your studies."_____
b "Honestly!"_____
c "It's really educational."_____
d "Nonsense!"_____
e "That's that." _____
f "It's not fair." _____

Individual speaking

Is it important to have interests outside schoolwork? Do you keep a good balance between your hobbies and your schoolwork? You are going to talk about this.

WB p60

Check-in

In detective fiction, somebody is trying to find out the answer to a puzzle or mystery. Sometimes, a crime has been committed and more crimes happen during the story.

Which famous detective character did Arthur Conan Doyle invent?
What other story or TV detectives do you know?
Would you be a good detective? Why? / Why not?

You are going to read an episode from a detective story. No crime has yet been committed, so far as we know …

Reading

- Luke has just flown to the airport. A security officer is watching the arrivals.

Why do airports have security officers?

- Before Luke meets his father, an officer asks Luke some **questions** about his luggage.

What questions do you think the officer might ask?

- A second officer **interviews** Luke.

What is the purpose of an interview?

- These words are in the story you are going to read.

stammer   passport   panic   hesitantly
burial   abruptly   insist

What do they mean? Check in a dictionary.

Looking at language

- Dictionary: **words with two or more meanings**.
- Spelling: **-ous**.
- Language development: **direct speech in fiction**.

What punctuation do you need for direct speech?

Grammar

- Practise **object pronouns, possessive pronouns, indirect object pronouns, possessive adjectives**.
- Practise **reflexives**: personal and for emphasis.
- Practise using *make* or *do*.

Writing

- Learn about the features of **detective stories**.
- Compose an investigative interview.
- Write an investigative interview.

Listening

- Jack and Holly's **conversation** about environmental disasters.
- A **TV programme** about an oil spill disaster.

Where do oil spills happen? How do they happen?

Speaking

- Talk with a partner about **environmental disasters**.
- Tell the class about an environmental disaster that you have researched yourself.

A desert map

Luke Terry has flown to visit his father, who is filming for a TV wildlife programme in the desert. As Luke went through the airport's immigration control, his passport was taken away and he was escorted to an interview room where a security officer asked him to open his suitcase.

"Did you pack this bag yourself?" The security officer gave Luke a hard stare.

"Yes," Luke replied nervously. He dropped his eyes under the man's hostile gaze.

"Did anyone give you anything to put in it?" he asked icily.

"No, … I … I mean, yes," Luke stammered.

"Which is it, yes or no?" the man hissed like a striking viper.

Luke felt himself break into a sweat. He tried to keep his voice even. He had no reason to feel guilty or afraid but he felt both. "My sister gave me a map."

"What map?" The man's eyes narrowed.

Luke pulled out the folded map of the desert that Miranda had given him just before he left London early that morning. Already it seemed like days ago. The officer took the map, opened it and looked at it silently.

"Look, can I go now? I just need my passport back, please. My father is meeting me, so I'd like to …" Even to Luke, his mumbled requests sounded feeble, nowhere near the assertive tone he had been aiming for.

"Wait," the officer snapped and left the room.

Luke felt nauseous. He tried to breathe deeply. There was no reason to panic, he told himself. He had done nothing wrong. His father was waiting for him in the arrivals hall. If the officer would just speak to his father, the problem, whatever it was, could be sorted out. Luke decided that he would suggest it as soon as the man came back.

He stood up with determination as the door opened but a different, smaller man walked into the room. "Well, Mr Luke Terry, aged seventeen from London," he said with a smile, "I have your passport here." Luke breathed a sigh of relief and reached out his hand to take it but the man made no move to give it to him. "First, I have just a few questions," he smiled again. "Please sit down … Now, Luke. What is the purpose of your visit?"

"I've come to stay with my father," Luke said hesitantly. "For the summer holidays," he added.

"Your father … what does he do?" the man enquired in a friendly tone.

"He's a cameraman … with a film company." Luke explained,

feeling his confidence returning. "They're filming desert wildlife. It takes months. So I'm staying with him while he's working. He's going to show me some of the places where they've been filming."

"So you're a tourist?" The man smiled at Luke encouragingly.

"Yes, that's right." Luke began to relax. He smiled at the man. The man smiled back. Then he leaned forward, no longer smiling, and spoke quietly. "Then why are you carrying a map with ancient secret burial sites marked on it?"

"I'm not … am I?" Luke gulped in amazement.

"I'm afraid you are. These sites are only known to a few people. How did you get that map?" the man asked sharply.

"My sister, Miranda, gave it to me," Luke told him.

"Is your sister an archaeologist?"

"An archaeologist! No, she's a student of zoology. She's mad about animals, like Dad."

"Then why did she mark the burial sites?"

"I don't know!" Luke's voice was raised in protest. "Look, she got the map in a second-hand bookshop. It must have been marked already."

The man smiled, shaking his head. "We've had a tip-off, you see. We've been waiting for a young man, about your age, to arrive from London, carrying a map of the desert. A marked map. Just like yours."

"Well, I'm not the person you're looking for," Luke insisted. "This map and these sites – they're nothing to do with me or my sister. It's just a map of the desert. That's all it is."

The man was completely silent. Suddenly he sat back in his chair. "I can see you're telling the truth," he said. "You're free to go. Enjoy your visit."

Astonished at being so abruptly released, Luke hurried out of the interview room and into the almost deserted arrival hall where his father was still waiting. "Luke!" he exclaimed. "What kept you?"

"They were asking me loads of weird questions, Dad. I'll tell you on the way."

As they weaved a way through the evening traffic towards the desert highway, Luke told his father about the interview. His father listened attentively. When Luke had finished, his father asked, "Have you still got the map?

"Yes. They let me keep it."

"That's interesting."

"Why?"

"Well, if the places were so secret, you'd think they'd have taken it away, wouldn't you?" Luke nodded in agreement. "So they must have had a reason," said his father thoughtfully. "I wonder what it is."

Luke frowned. "So do I," he said.

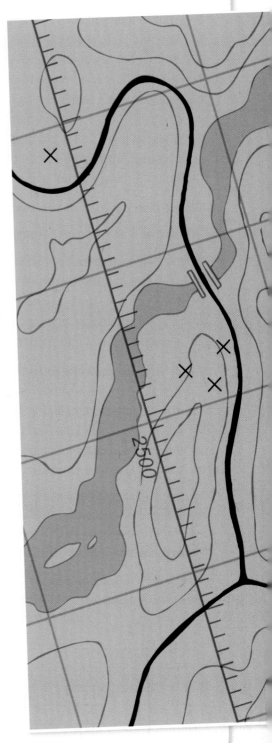

Reading comprehension

1   Answer these questions.

1   What has Luke been asked to do when the story starts?
2   What is the map of?
3   What did Luke decide that he would suggest to the officer?
4   Why did the second man not give Luke his passport straight away?
5   How long has Luke come to stay with his father for?
6   What is Luke's father filming?
7   What was marked on the map?
8   What is Luke's sister studying at the moment?
9   What was special about the bookshop where Miranda bought the map?
10   What did Luke's father expect the officers to do with a very secret map?

2   Find these phrases in the text. Match them to the definitions below.

> weave a way   tip-off   immigration control   security officer   second-hand

1   the place where people arriving in a country have their passports checked
2   a person whose job is to ensure the safety of a building or place
3   having already been owned by another person
4   to go by a bending, curving route that goes around other objects
5   a piece of useful information often given secretly

If you don't know the whole phrase, think about the meanings of the words that you already know.

3   Discuss your answers to these questions.

1   Can you explain why the first officer asked Luke if he packed the bag himself?
2   How does Luke feel during the interview? How do you know?
3   Why do you think Luke feels like that?
4   Why do you think the second man released Luke so suddenly?
5   Why do you think Luke was allowed to keep the map?

Vocabulary check

Find these words in the text and read the sentence where each one appears. Categorise them into word classes and list the words for each class.

> escort   hostile   stammer   viper   even   guilty   passport   mumble   feeble   assertive   tone   aim for
> snap   nauseous   panic   sort out   suggest   determination   hesitantly   relax   burial   gulp   sharply
> raise   protest   insist   abruptly   deserted   weird   highway   attentively

_____   _____
_____   _____
_____   _____
_____   _____
_____   _____

Your views

- How would you feel if you were asked questions by a security officer at an airport? Why?
- Do you think Luke is brave or easily scared?
- Would you have done or said anything differently to Luke? Explain your answer.

A Dictionary work
Words with two or more meanings 1

- Some words have **more than one meaning** even though they are the **same part of speech**.

officer /ˈɒfɪsə/ *noun* [C] **1** someone in a position of power and authority in the armed forces: *an army officer* **2** a police officer **3** someone with a position of authority in an organisation

1 Choose the correct definition for each word as it is used on page 68.

1 feeble a physically weak
b not strong enough to be seen or heard clearly
2 room a part of a building with a floor, walls and a ceiling
b the amount of space needed for a particular purpose
3 company a an organisation that sells services or goods
b the activity of being with other people

2 Each of these words has two meanings for the same part of speech. Write two sentences for each word using the different meanings.

1 eighth 2 gown
3 nursery 4 painter

B Spelling
-ous

The ending *-ous* is used:
- with a root word ending in a consonant.
  danger – dangerous
- to create an adverb from a root word ending in a silent e.
  nerve – nervous
- If a root word ends in *-f*, it changes to *-v* before *-ous* is added. *grief – grievous*
- If a root word ends in *-our*, drop the *-u-* before adding *-ous*. *humour – humorous*

1 Follow the rules and add *-ous* to each of these words.

1 ridicule 2 carnivore 3 fame
4 mischief 5 glamour 6 mountain

2 Choose three of the *-ous* words you have made and use them in sentences of your own.

C Language development
Direct speech in fiction

- *said* is the most commonly used word for reporting direct speech. It is often appropriate, especially when a character is speaking in a normal tone of voice.
  "That's my book," she said.
- There are many other verbs that express the way in which a person spoke.
  1 *"That's my book," she whispered.*
  2 *"That's my book," she shouted.*
  3 *"That's my book," she sobbed.*

1 Match these adjectives to the speaker in each sentence above: *unhappy, scared, annoyed*.

2 Read the sentences aloud with the right expression in the spoken words.

- **Reporting verbs** are important because they can tell the reader how someone is feeling.
- They can also express what someone is doing when they speak.
  "Look at the clown," he laughed.
- They can also be used to present a character's personality and behaviour.

3 *Snap, mumble, insist* and *stammer* are reporting verbs. Which ones express forceful speech and which ones express hesitant speech?

4 Read these sentences. Then read them aloud with the correct expression.
"Open your bag," snapped the officer. "Do it at once," he insisted.
"I … I can't" Meg stammered. "I haven't got the key," she mumbled.

- Reporting words can also help to express the relationship between two people.

5 In the sentences above, who is the most powerful character?

- The reporting words can change characters' behaviour and the whole situation.

6 Read these sentences with expression.
"Open your bag," mumbled the officer. "D … Do it at once," he stammered.
"I can't," Meg snapped. "I haven't got the key," she insisted.

7 Now who is the most powerful?

Grammar

1 Read.

"**I** have **your** passport here," said the man. Luke reached out **his** hand to take **it** but the man made no move to give **it** to **him**.

"What is the purpose of **your** visit?" **he** asked.

"**I**'ve come to stay with my father," Luke replied. "**He**'s a cameraman with a film company. **They**'re filming wildlife in the desert."

"Where did **you** get this map?" the man asked quietly.

"**My** sister Miranda gave **it** to **me**", said Luke. "**She** bought **it** in a second-hand shop."

"**We**'re very interested in maps of the desert, especially marked maps just like **yours**," the man said.

The man was silent for a while and then suddenly said, "**You**'re free to go." Astonished, Luke hurried into the arrival hall where **his** father was still waiting.

"Luke!" **he** exclaimed. "What kept **you**?"

"**They** were asking **me** loads of weird questions," said Luke.

2 Answer these questions.

1. Why did the man refuse to give Luke his passport?
2. What was the purpose of Luke's visit?
3. Why was his father in that country?
4. How had Luke come by the map?
5. Where had his sister found it?
6. How did Luke explain his late arrival to his father?

3

Remember!

The subject pronouns are: *I, you, he, she, it, we, you, they*
She likes sailing. We enjoy swimming. They like football.
Direct and indirect object pronouns have the same form: *me, you, him, her, it, us, you, them*
Direct object pronouns:
I saw him. He saw me. We saw them.
Indirect object pronouns:
He gave the flowers to her. He gave her the flowers. He gave them to her. He gave her them.

Ask and answer in pairs.

1. Did she give the present to her father?
   Yes, she gave it to him.
2. Did they show the photo to their mother?
3. Did you send the postcards to your grandfather?
4. Did she buy the sweets for you and me?
5. Did they recommend that man for the job?
6. Did you tell the story to the children?

4

Remember!

The possessive adjectives are: my, your, his, her, its, our, your, their
My friends invited me to their house.
A horse was in the field with its foal.
The possessive pronouns are: mine, yours, his, hers, ours, yours, theirs
"Is this your coat?" "Yes, it's mine."
"Are these Jenny's books?" "Yes, they're hers."

Complete these sentences with possessive adjectives which match the underlined words.

1. My sister and I would like to introduce you to _____ parents.
2. The size of the building and _____ design astonished us.
3. Please hand me back _____ passport.
4. Can you tell me where you bought _____ map?
5. Luke knew that _____ father was waiting for him.
6. They weaved _____ way through the traffic.

5 Answer the questions using possessive pronouns.

1. Is that Luke's passport?
   Yes, it's his.
2. Are these your sunglasses?
3. Do these CDs belong to you and your friend?
4. Does that house belong to your grandparents?
5. Are these Maria's photos?
6. Are you sure this money belongs to me?

*Saturday 6pm
Brad online
(10am in Vancouver)*

1

🎧 **2.02 Listen and read.**

Holly: Hi, Brad! It's brilliant to talk to you like this.

Brad: You want to know about the *Exxon Valdez*, right? I don't know much about it **myself** but I'll try and help.

Jack: We're doing a feature on pollution of the oceans.

Brad: Great topic! Excellent!

Holly: It was Jack's idea. He's feeling very pleased with **himself**!

Holly: When did the disaster happen, Brad?

Brad: In 1989, before I was born but my parents have told me about it.

Jack: It happened off the coast of Canada, didn't it?

Brad: No, it happened in Alaska. That's part of the USA but pretty close to where I live. The *Exxon Valdez* was an oil tanker. It hit some rocks and a huge amount of oil spilled into the ocean. It caused terrible damage.

Jack: These oil companies … They should be ashamed of **themselves**. Disasters like this happen too often.

Holly: Hang on, Jack. Maybe it was an accident. Accidents happen.

Brad: My dad helped with the clean-up operation.

Holly: Really? Can you ask him about it for us?

Brad: Why don't you speak to him **yourselves**? He'd be happy to help.

2 Answer these questions.

1 Where is Brad from?
2 What are Jack and Holly doing a feature on?
3 Why is Jack feeling pleased with himself?
4 What was the *Exxon Valdez*?
5 What happened to it?
6 When and where did the disaster happen?
7 How was Brad's father involved?
8 What does Brad suggest?

3 Complete these sentences with reflexive pronouns.

1 Jane is looking at _____ in the mirror.
2 Laura and Jack enjoyed _____ on holiday.
3 You've done well, Holly. You should be proud of _____.
4 The horse hurt _____ when it tried to jump the fence.
5 I must remind _____ to buy that book.
6 We're cold and tired and feel very sorry for _____.
7 After behaving so badly, Joe felt ashamed of _____.
8 All you young people must take care of _____ in New York.

4 Add reflexive pronouns to these sentences.

1 The president _____ paid our school a visit.

2 Everyone's talking about this film. I _____ don't think much of it.
3 Lucy knows a lot about China but she _____ has never been there.
4 You won the match, boys, but you _____ know that you were lucky.
5 Alaska has a border with Canada but the state _____ is actually part of the USA.
6 Nobody, not even the oil companies _____, can prevent all accidents.

5

Remember!

Reflexive pronouns

myself, yourself, himself, herself, itself, ourselves, yourselves, themselves

We use them when the direct object (or indirect object) is the same person as the subject.

*John hurt **himself**.*
*She asked **herself** a question.*
*You must look after **yourselves**.*

We use them to give extra emphasis to a pronoun or noun.

*She cut her hair **herself**.*
*The boys made the cake **themselves**.*
*I **myself** don't agree with you.*
*We caught sight of **the pyramid itself**.*

Find examples of reflexive pronouns in the dialogue.

▶ *Grammar extra p129*

Writing

Features of detective writing

> At some point in a detective story there is an interview. Questions are asked to find out important information. In *A Desert Map* Luke is questioned by two officers at the airport about a map. We find out a lot about the characters of the two men and Luke through what they say and how they say it.

▶ **Plot and setting**

All stories have a **plot** and **setting**.

> Discuss the extract:
> * a the **plot** – what happens?
> * b the **setting** – where does it happen?

▶ **Character and dialogue**

We learn about characters in stories through how the author describes them and what they do. We can also learn a lot about the characters through **dialogue**. The first officer who questions Luke has a 'hard stare' and a 'hostile gaze'. The author tells us he:

| asked icily | hissed like a striking viper | snapped |

Luke:

| replied nervously | stammered | mumbled |

The second officer:

| smiled | spoke quietly | asked sharply |

> Discuss each of the **characters**. Use the **quotes** above and any others you can find in the extract to help you form an **impression** of the three characters.

▶ **Synonyms for *said***

The author uses words instead of *said* – **synonyms** – to show how characters speak.

| "No … I … I mean yes," Luke **stammered**. | "Which is it, yes or no?" the man **hissed** like a striking viper. |

> Read the first five lines of the extract using *said* instead of the author's words. Does that make it easier to form **an impression** of Luke and the officer, or more difficult? Explain your reasons.

▶ **Punctuating direct speech**

Direct speech is when we write the exact words a character says.
The spoken words begin and end with **speech marks**.

> "First, I have a few questions," he smiled.

Punctuation at the end of the spoken words comes before the speech marks.

> "So, you're a tourist?" the man smiled at Luke encouragingly.

The words that tell you **who** is speaking can come at the beginning or at the end of the sentence.

| "I've come to stay with my father," **Luke said hesitantly**. | **Luke said hesitantly**, "I've come to stay with my father." |

Sometimes the words that tell you who is speaking can come in the **middle**.

"I can see that you're telling the truth," he said. "You're free to go."

ACTIVITY
Copy these sentences. Put in the missing **punctuation**.
1 I think that's the boy we're looking for said the first officer.
2 Who is he asked the second officer.
3 His name's Luke Terry he replied. He's seventeen and from London.
4 The second officer smiled. I think we better ask him some questions.

The interview

Interviews in detective stories are not just a pleasant chat! The person asking the questions (the interviewer) needs to find out information. The person answering the questions (the interviewee) either doesn't know the answers or won't tell!

Discuss:
1 What do the two officers want to know?
2 Do you think Luke is telling the truth? Does he know about the 'ancient secret burial sites' or not?
3 Do you believe the second officer when he says "I can see you're telling the truth"?
4 The interview hasn't given the officers the information they want. What do you think they will do now?

Writing together

As a class, you are going to continue the extract from *A Desert Map*. You are going to write a telephone conversation Luke had with his sister, Miranda, about the map. Luke was nervous and frightened in his interview, and Miranda is a new character that the reader has not met yet.

Things to think about.

- How does Luke begin the conversation?
  Does he chat about lots of things or ask about the map straight away?

- Questions he asks his sister:
  Did she mark the map?
  Did she notice the marks on the map?
  Where exactly did she buy the map?
  Has she bought things there before?
  What was the shopkeeper like?

- Is Luke still as nervous and frightened as before? Is he now curious and excited about the mystery? Is he bored and uninterested?

- Is Miranda interested in what Luke is telling her? Is she horrified or uncaring about his experience at the airport? Does she answer Luke's questions as fully as possible or think he is making a fuss about nothing?

Write the conversation.

Remember!
- You can decide how much Miranda knows or does not know about the map.
- Think carefully about the **questions** and **answers**. Luke wants as much **information** as possible from his sister.
- Use **synonyms for *said*** to help the reader understand the characters and how they are feeling.
- Set out the **direct speech** correctly.

WB p70

Conversation practice

1 Jack and Holly are talking. Look at the pictures and the words in the box. What do you think they are talking about?

> environmental disaster   man-made   natural   oil spill   pollution
> contaminated   volcanic eruption   red-hot lava   ash cloud
> flood   burst … banks   earthquake   severe   loss of life

2 🎧 2.03 **Listen to Jack and Holly. Were you right?**

3 🎧 2.03 **Listen again. Which disasters do they consider man-made and which do they consider natural?**

4 Talk with your friends about environmental disasters.
Start like this: *Environmental disasters seem to happen all the time, don't they?*

Listening comprehension

1 🎧 2.04 **Listen to part of a TV programme about the *Exxon Valdez* disaster.**

2 🎧 2.04 **Read the statements. They are all false. Listen again and underline the mistakes. Then correct the mistakes.**

1   The *Exxon Valdez* set out on 23rd May, 1998.
2   The ship was heading for Alaska.
3   The tanker was carrying 65 million gallons of oil.
4   The ship's captain followed his usual course.
5   The ship crashed into an iceberg.
6   All the ship's cargo spilled into the ocean.
7   Only a few Alaskan residents helped with the clean-up operation.
8   Approximately half a million seabirds were killed.
9   There was an increase in the numbers of fish in the area.
10 Over twenty years later the region has managed to recover.

3 **What do you know about the disaster which you didn't know before? Talk with your friends.**

Individual speaking

You are going to research and talk about an environmental disaster.   WB p71 ▶

In my view

Check-in

People have opinions about all sorts of things.
Often people's opinions about a single topic vary.
When people have different opinions, they debate
their views.

List two things you have a strong opinion about.
Whose opinions do you most often disagree with?
Do you send your opinions to magazines or websites?
Have you ever taken part in a school debate?

You are going to read the results of a magazine survey.

Reading

* In the **survey**, people give their opinions about text
  messaging.

Do you use text messaging? For what purposes?

* The survey was done for *Language Magazine*.

What do you think some of the opinions
about text messaging will be?

* These words are in the opinions you are going to
  read.

  inappropriate   convention   analyse
  disgruntled   ability   manage

What do they mean? Check in a dictionary.

Looking at language

* Dictionary: **words with two or more meanings**.
* Spelling: *-ise / -ize / -yse*.
* Language development: **pronouns**.

Grammar

* Practise **reported questions with tense shifts**;
  if / whether + **question words**.
* Practise **exclamations**: *what, what a, so, such a,
  such*; **result clauses** *so ... that*.
* Practise **phrases with *make***.

Writing

* Learn about the features of **writing about opinion**.
* Write different opinions about a subject.
* Collect and write about different opinions.

Listening

* Ross and Jack's **conversation** about losing things.
* **Monologues** describing items that people have lost.

Speaking

* Talk with a partner about **something you have lost**.
* Tell the class about an event when something
  valuable was lost.

Language Magazine

Text messaging – GR8 or not?

Language Magazine recently conducted a survey asking people about text messaging. Those taking part were asked if they used text messaging, and what effect they thought it was having on the standard of English used by young people.

Of the people surveyed, 48% used text messaging; 51% thought it made the standard of young people's English worse; 49% thought it made no difference.

Here is a sample of the replies showing widely differing opinions.

I am particularly concerned about text messaging because of the harmful effect it has on young people's spelling. Of course, many of my pupils are fully aware that 'b4' is fine in a text message but is inappropriate in a piece of schoolwork. More problematic is the text messaging convention of using a capital letter to represent double letters in a word e.g. tomoRow and lOking. Fewer pupils realise that this is actually wrong and it creeps into their written English. But even this convention seems to be disappearing and 'tomorow', 'loking', etc. is becoming the norm. **Anna**

Why are we getting so worked up about text messaging? Why do we assume that it is just a teenage craze? It is, in fact, a recognised means of communicating in business. Billions of text messages are sent each year by adults who find it quick and easy to use, and can't imagine how they ever managed without it. I know I do. Don't you?
Ahmed Eid

I have always had a bee in my bonnet about punctuation. Without it, written English can be rendered meaningless. The fact that punctuation is used in text messages solely to draw little pictures – :-) = I'm happy, is ridiculous. No capital letters! No full stops! It is so difficult to make out what the message is! I'm sure you have the same problem.
Aimee

Let's analyse why those who use text messaging see it as an advantageous means of communication. Firstly, in my opinion, it is such a quick and immediate way of passing on information, asking and responding to questions and making arrangements that it is obviously here to stay. Secondly, it is very private – more private than the telephone where anyone in the vicinity can hear at least one side of the conversation. You have to admit – these are very positive advantages. **Jiffen Patel**

My major concern is the very limited vocabulary needed to be proficient at texting. Feelings are expressed using smiley or disgruntled yellow faces or 'emoticons'. The rich and varied content of the English language is limited to a few stock phrases, and young people are losing the ability to express themselves in any way other than 'GR8' and 'H8'! **Maria Ferreira**

Text messaging is here to stay. More and more young people have mobile phones and choose texting as a quick, efficient means of communicating. Some people want to ban text messaging! What a ridiculous notion! What we have to do is to ensure that young people know that the language and conventions of texting, with all their abbreviations, missing punctuation and odd spellings, are appropriate only for texting and should not be used in any other form of written communication. We won't do that by trying – and failing – to ban it. As adults, one of the main reasons we don't like the idea is that to many of us it is 'strange' and 'new'. So, learn about it, be willing to use it appropriately, and then you can advise young people how to use it wisely and selectively.
Sara Evans

Reading comprehension

1   Who is ...

1   ... worried that text messaging limits vocabulary?
2   ... aware that many adults use text messaging?
3   ... in favour of text messaging because it is 'quick' and 'efficient'?
4   ... concerned that text messaging affects spelling?
5   ... convinced text messaging is here to stay?
6   ... annoyed by the lack of punctuation in text messaging?

2   Match each of these expressions to the correct meaning.

> fully aware   teenage craze   worked up   ridiculous notion
> bee in my bonnet   stock phrases   here to stay   rendered meaningless

1   irritated / angry   2   completely understand
3   made totally unclear   4   continue to exist for a long time
5   popular with young people   6   simple, unoriginal expressions
7   silly idea   8   think something is very important

3   Find these adjectives in the survey replies. Match each adjective to its correct meaning.

> appropriate   problematic   advantageous   proficient   efficient

1   likely to make someone or something more successful   2   suitable for a particular situation
3   involving or causing problems   4   working well and producing good results
5   very good at something

4   Discuss your answers.

1   Which of the writers do you think is: a a teacher?   b a businessman?
    Find evidence in the text to support your answers.
2   Explain in your own words why Maria Ferreira thinks text messaging limits vocabulary.
3   According to the writers, what are the advantages and disadvantages of text messaging?
4   Which of the writers sees both sides of the argument?

Vocabulary check

Find these words in the survey replies. Check any you are not sure of in a dictionary.

survey (n)	inappropriate (adj)	convention (n)	assuming (vb)
communication (n)	rendered (vb)	vicinity (n)	emoticons (n)
notion (n)	recently (adv)	selectively (adv)	represent (vb)
norm (n)	solely (adv)	analyse (vb)	varied (adj)
ability (n)	disgruntled (adj)	billions (n)	manage (vb)
immediate (adj)	obviously (adv)	limited (adj)	

Your views

- Which of the writers' views do you agree with?
- Which do you disagree with?
- What, in your opinion, is:
    a the major advantage of text messaging?
    b the major disadvantage of text messaging?
- Explain your reasons.

> You can agree / disagree with more than one viewpoint.

A Dictionary work
Words with two or more meanings 2

- In Unit 7, we looked at words with **two or more meanings** for the **same part of speech**.
- Some words have **two or more meanings** because they are **different parts of speech**.

> **text**[1] /tekst/ *noun* [U] the part of a book, magazine, or computer document that consists of writing and not pictures
>
> **text**[2] /tekst/ *verb* [T] to send a written message to someone using a mobile phone

1   **Look up these words in a dictionary. Say what two parts of speech each word can be.**

   coat   heap   rap   sketch   uniform

2   **Choose three of the words in Activity 1 and write sentences to show their meanings for each part of speech. Here is an example:**

noun = *I read the **text** carefully.*
verb = *He **texted** his friend.*

B Spelling
-ise / -ize / -yse

> *Some dictionaries give both spellings. Some do not.*

- Some words in English have the ending *-ise*.
  *… we can **advise** young people …*
- There are a group of words that have been traditionally spelt with the ending *-ise* but, more and more, *-ize* is accepted.
  *Fewer pupils **realize** [realise] …*
- A small group of words have the ending *-yse*.
  *Let's **analyse** why those who use text messaging …*

1   **Use a dictionary and complete each word with -ise / -ize or -yse.**

   1 adv_____   2 paral_____   3 critic_____

   4 enterpr_____   5 recogn_____   6 surpr_____

2   **Match each word with its correct definition. Use a dictionary to help you.**

   improvise   emphasise   synchronise

   1   give particular importance or attention to something
   2   to make two or more things happen at the same time
   3   do something without any preparation

C Language development
Pronouns

- A pronoun stands in place of a noun.
- A pronoun is often used to refer back to a noun that has previously been mentioned.
  *The magazine always had interesting articles and **it** was read by thousands of people every week.*

> *Quick revision.*

1   **What does *it* refer to in the sentence above?**

- This use avoids repeating the noun and helps to make a sentence shorter and quicker to read and understand.

2   **What does *it* refer to in the sentences below? Write the noun at the end of each sentence.**

   1   I am particularly concerned about text messaging because of the effect it has on young people's spelling. _____
   2   I have always had a bee in my bonnet about punctuation. Without it, written English can be rendered meaningless. _____

Missing pronouns

- A pronoun can be omitted from a sentence when it is the subject of a main clause after a conjunction and the subject of the second clause is the same as the first.
  Of course, many of my pupils are fully aware that 'b4' is fine in a text message but is inappropriate in a piece of schoolwork.

3   **Answer these questions about the sentence above.**

   1   Which pronoun is missing? _____
   2   What would the complete sentence be if the pronoun was included?
   3   What noun does the pronoun replace? _____

Missing nouns

- Sometimes a noun can be omitted where it goes before a conjunction and can be understood from the rest of the sentence.
  *Feelings are expressed using smiley **or** disgruntled yellow faces.*

4   **What noun does *smiley* describe in the sentence above?** _____

Grammar

1 Read.

Language Magazine recently conducted a survey asking people about text messaging. First they **asked** those taking part **if** they **used** text messages. If the answer was yes, they **wanted to know what** people **liked** or disliked about it. They also **asked whether** text messaging **should be** banned in schools.

Some of those taking part in the survey did not approve of text messaging. One teacher **wondered if** text messaging **was having** a bad effect on her pupil's spelling. Another lady **asked why** young people only **used** punctuation to draw little pictures.

Some people were in favour of text messaging. One person said that it was not just a teenage craze. He **wondered how** business people **had** ever **managed** without it. Another person liked the privacy of text messaging. He **asked** which **was** more private, a phone call or a text message?

> What do people like or dislike about it?

> Should text messaging be banned in schools?

> Is text messaging having a bad effect on my pupils' spelling?

> Why do young people only use punctuation to draw little pictures?

> Which is more private, a phone call or a text message?

> How did business people ever manage without it?

2 Answer these questions.

1 What was the topic of the *Language Magazine* survey?
2 What did they ask first?
3 What else did they want to know?
4 What else did they ask?
5 Did everyone approve of text messaging? Why not?
6 Why did those in favour of text messaging like it?

3 Report the questions. Use the words in brackets. Don't change any tenses.

1 "Are the students in the library?" (Jane wants to know if …)
   Jane wants to know if the students are in the library.
2 "Does Billy speak Spanish?" (She is asking whether …)
3 "Has Holly lost her mobile?" (Ross wants to know if …)
4 "Can Jack finish his work?" (The teacher is wondering if …)
5 "Did Laura see the film?" (Holly is asking whether …)
6 "Where are the students?" (The teacher is asking …)
7 "When does the exam start?" (I wonder …)
8 "How is Laura feeling?" (Holly wants to know …)
9 "Where did Laura go?" (The teacher wants to know …)
10 "What is that animal?" (Laura is wondering …)

4 Report these questions. Change the tenses. Make other changes if necessary.

1 "Where is your mobile, Laura?" asked Jack.
   Jack asked Laura where her mobile was.
2 Brad asked, "Do you speak French, Holly?"
3 "What are you doing, Ross?" Holly asked.
4 "How can I help?" Laura wondered.
5 "When will the exam start?" the boy wanted to know.
6 "Did you finish your work, Ross?" Laura asked.

Remember!
Reported questions
- You can use *if* or *whether*.
  "Is the phone working?" ⟶ *He wants to know if / whether the phone is working.*
- You can use a question word (**what, who, why, how**, etc.)
  "When are the exams?" ⟶ *Susie asked when the exams were.*
- If the reporting verb is in the present tense, we don't change the tense of the verb in the direct speech. (See the first example above.)
- If the reporting verb is in the past tense, we often change the tense of the verb in the direct speech. (See the second example above.)
- Sometimes you need to change pronouns, too. There are no question marks in reported questions.
- **Be very careful about word order!**

1 🎧 (2.06) Listen and read.

Holly: Ross? Ross? Is that you?

Ross: Holly? What's the matter?

Holly: Something terrible's happened. I'm in **such a** panic!

Ross: Try to calm down. What's the problem?

Holly: I've lost it. I've lost the project. It was all on the memory stick and now it's gone. All our work has disappeared!

Ross: Oh dear. **How** annoying!

Holly: Annoying? Annoying? It's disastrous! I'm **so** angry with myself I could scream.

Ross: What happened exactly?

Holly: I don't know. I was in a rush. I was working **so** fast **that** I wasn't concentrating properly. **What a** stupid, stupid thing to do!

Ross: Take it easy. It's not the end of the world.

Holly: But it is! It is! Why do I do **such** silly things?

Ross: Don't worry. Everything'll be OK.

Holly: How can you stay **so** calm?

Ross: Because there's someone who I'm sure can help. Laura! She's our computer expert.

Holly: But Laura's left the project. She hasn't got time for this.

Ross: She'll make time. This is an emergency! Don't worry!

2 Cover the dialogue and say if the following statements are true or false. Check your answers. Correct the false statements.

1 Holly is feeling fine today.
2 Holly is calmer than Ross.
3 The project was on a memory stick.
4 She lost the work because she was working too slowly.
5 There is no one who can help.

3 Remember!

How + adjective / adverb:

How beautiful! How beautifully they sing!

What a / an + countable noun:

What a great day! What an exciting race!

What + plural noun:

What charming children! What fast cars!

What + uncountable noun:

What delicious food! What terrible news!

What + abstract noun:

What elegance! What intolerable heat!

Make exclamations. Use *How, What a / an* or *What*.

1 interesting opinions
2 fascinating survey
3 horrible
4 fast he drives
5 terrible punctuation
6 exciting project

4 Remember!

so + adjective / adverb:

The music is so loud! He speaks so loudly!

such a / an + countable noun:

He's such a nice man! It's such an interesting book!

such + plural noun:

They're such hard-working students!

such + uncountable noun:

This is such tasteless soup!

such + abstract noun:

I have never seen such appalling behaviour!

Think of different ways to finish the exclamations.

1 The mountain is so …
2 This is such a …
3 These are such …
4 The choir sings so …

5 Remember!

- You can use *so, such a / an* and *such* in **result clauses**.

  We drove so fast that we soon arrived home.

  It was such a good film that I saw it three times.

- You can omit *that* in all the sentences above.

  She's shown such kindness I'll never forget her.

Think of different ways to finish the exclamations.

1 violent storm
2 softly
3 terrible fear
4 difficult

Grammar extra p129 ▶

Writing

Features of writing about opinions

> **The survey in *Language Magazine* is the result of asking people their opinion of text messaging. People gave their opinion and their reasons.**

▶ **Introduction**

When you are expressing your own **opinion**, or asking other people for theirs, it must be very clear to the reader what is being discussed **from the beginning**.

> *Language Magazine* recently conducted a survey asking people about text messaging.

ACTIVITY
What other **useful information** does the introduction give the reader?

Gr8!

▶ **First person**

Each person who has contributed to the survey is expressing his or her opinion in the **first person**.

> *I* have always had a bee in my bonnet about punctuation.

> Firstly, in **my** opinion ...

ACTIVITY
Change these **third person** sentences into **first person** sentences.
1 He has lost his mobile phone.
2 The text message didn't come through so she didn't know what time they were meeting.
3 She was careful not to use any texting conventions in her schoolwork.

▶ **Reasons**

If the magazine article said, 'Some people like text messaging and some people don't' then it would be very short and the reader would have learned nothing!
The **reasons** people give for their opinions are very important.

> the harmful effect it has on young people's spelling.

> it is such a quick and easy way of passing on information ...

ACTIVITY
Re-read the survey. Find:
a two more arguments **against** text messaging.
b two more arguments **in favour of** text messaging.

▶ **Second person**

Someone expressing an opinion will often use the **second person** to get the reader involved.

> **You** have to admit ...

> I'm sure **you** have the same problem.

ACTIVITY
Find another example of the **second person** in the survey.

▶ **Questions**

Questions are used for the same reason as the second person – they get the reader involved and give them something to think about.

> I know I do. Don't you?

> 'Why are we getting so worked up about text messaging?'

ACTIVITY
Find another example of a **question** in the survey.

▶ **Persuasive language**

When you express an opinion you often want people to agree with you.

The words you choose can be very **persuasive**.

Anna is not just slightly worried. She is '**particularly concerned**'.

Aimee doesn't just think that the lack of punctuation is annoying. She thinks that without it written English is '**rendered meaningless**' and that it is '**ridiculous**!'

<table>
<tr><td>ACTIVITY</td><td>Find three other examples in the survey of **persuasive language**.</td></tr>
</table>

Writing together

As a class, you are going to choose a subject that students have different opinions about. Discuss the reasons for those different opinions. Write four short letters like the ones you have studied in *Language Magazine*. Each letter must express opinion and give reasons.

Here are some suggestions:

Football is a silly game!

All cars should be banned from city centres.

Children under ten years of age should not be allowed to watch TV.

Choose one of the above suggestions or agree on another subject.

Remember!
- Make it clear what the survey is about in your **introduction**.
- Each person is expressing his/her opinion so use **the first person**.
- Use some examples of **second person, questions** and **persuasive language** to get the reader involved.

WB p79

Conversation practice

1 **Ross and Jack are talking. Look at the pictures and the words in the box. What do you think they are talking about?**

> laptop files save delete pickpocket locked out
> ringtone engagement ring missing forgetful

2 **🎧 2.07 Listen to Ross and Jack. Were you right?**

3 **🎧 2.07 Read the phrases in the box. Listen again and spot the phrases.**

> How on earth ...? by mistake What a shame!
> What a nuisance! tracked it down run in the family

4 **Talk with your friends about things which you or members of your family have lost.**

Start like this: *Have you ever lost anything on the computer?*

Listening comprehension

1 **🎧 2.08 Look at the pictures. These people have lost some items. Listen and match the people to their belongings.**

2 **🎧 2.08 Read these questions. Listen again and answer the questions.**

1 What does the woman think happened to her item?
2 Explain how the teenage boy lost his item.
3 Why is the girl's mother going to be furious?
4 Why was the older lady carrying her item in the street?
5 Why might you regret picking up the man's item?

Individual speaking

Have you, or someone you know, ever lost something important or valuable? You are going to describe what happened.

> WB p80

What a wonder!

Check-in

The original Seven Wonders were in the Ancient World and existed thousands of years ago. In modern times people have compiled lists of new and natural wonders.

> *What were the Seven Wonders of the Ancient World?*
> *Which of them still exists?*
> *What special places are there in your country?*
> *List remarkable buildings or natural places.*

You are going to read a magazine article about the Wonders of the United Kingdom.

Reading

- The Wonders of the United Kingdom were chosen in a competition that was organised by a national newspaper. People were invited to vote online.

> *How many people do you think voted?*

- The magazine article **describes** each 'wonder'.
- The article is set out with **sub-headings** and **paragraphs**.

> *Why is the article set out in this way?*
> *What else would you expect to see included on the magazine pages?*

- These words are in the article you are going to read.
> *location   summit   prehistoric   residence*
> *destination   fatalities*

> *What do they mean? Check in a dictionary.*

Looking at language

- Dictionary: **words with two or more meanings**.
- Spelling: **words ending -ary / -ery / -ory**.

> *Think of a word with each of these endings.*

- Language development: **clause order; prefix over-**.

Grammar

- Practise **present continuous passive**, **past continuous passive**.
- Practise **adjective + preposition**, e.g. *keen on*.
- Practise **phrases with *talk***.

Writing

- Learn about the **features of magazine articles**.
- Write a magazine article from given notes.
- Research and write you own magazine article.

Listening

- Laura and Ross's **discussion** of a healthy diet.
- Holly and Jack's **questionnaire answers**.

Speaking

- Talk with a partner **about eating a healthy diet**.
- Tell the class about your own diet and how healthy it is.

And the winners are ...

Do you like entering competitions? Sometimes you can win a prize; sometimes you can vote for your favourite person, place or thing and the one with the most votes is the winner.

A competition to find not one, but several 'Wonders of the United Kingdom' was organised by a national newspaper, and there was an overwhelming response. In the first stage, people went online and made suggestions. Twenty-five locations were then chosen, and by the third stage people had fourteen from which to make their final selection. In all, over twenty million people voted in the competition and here are some of the most popular places that include natural, historical and cultural treasures.

Hampton Court

The palace and grounds of Hampton Court are located in Greater London and are one of the city's most popular attractions. Built as a manor house in the 11th century and remodelled as a palace by Henry VIII, many say that this was the King's favourite residence.

The palace is surrounded by a breathtaking estate that is famous for its maze. It was designed by George London and Henry Wise around 1700, and extends over 1,350sq m. People enjoy getting lost in it and you can wander around the narrow paths for ages without finding your way out.

Stonehenge

Situated on Salisbury Plain in the county of Wiltshire, Stonehenge is a prehistoric monument. It is a circle of large standing stones. It was begun around 5,500 years ago and added to over a 2,000-year period.

We know that it was being used initially as a burial site but what other uses it had remain a mystery. Just as puzzling is how the Bluestone, Sarsen and Welsh Sandstone were carried over colossal distances to the site.

As well as Stonehenge itself, the area has a number of other important prehistoric sites. It covers an area of 800 hectares and became a World Heritage Site in 1986. It will continue to be visited and studied for many years to come. Plans are being drawn up to provide a new visitors' centre, 2.5km from the Standing Stones.

Ben Nevis

This majestic peak, standing at 1,344m, is the highest point in Great Britain. It is situated in the Grampian Range of mountains in Scotland. The name *Ben Nevis* translates from the Scottish Gaelic as 'the mountain with its head in the clouds'.

The first recorded ascent of Ben Nevis was made on 17th August, 1771, by James Robertson. The mountain is still a popular destination for climbers today and 100,000 people make an attempt to reach the summit each year. The steep and rocky sides, together with year-round snow and fog, lead to a high number of mountain rescues. In 1999, for example, there were forty-one rescues and four fatalities.

Castle Howard

This building in Yorkshire is considered one of the grandest private houses in the United Kingdom. Construction began in 1699 and was completed in 1712 for the Earl of Carlisle. It was designed by John Vanburgh.

The castle has 145 rooms, 1,000 acres of gardens and a lake. Since it opened to the public in 1999, it is not only popular with tourists – 230,000 visited in 2009 – it is also a popular setting for films and TV programmes.

Wastwater

Situated in the Lake District National Park, Wastwater holds many national records. It is 4.6km long and 600m wide. At 79m, it is the deepest lake in England. It is encircled by mountains including England's highest peak, Scafell Pike showing scree. For this reason, it is a very popular place for climbers.

In 2007, Wastwater was voted the winner of a television competition to find 'Britain's Favourite View'.

The Giant's Causeway

The Giant's Causeway can be found on the north-east coast of Northern Ireland and is one of the United Kingdom's most extraordinary attractions. There are about 40,000 basalt columns, resulting from an ancient volcanic eruption. The tallest of the columns is about 12m high.

The Giant's Causeway became a popular tourist attraction in the 19th century and remains so to this day. Visitors can actually walk over these extraordinary columns that are the home for seabirds such as the cormorant and razorbill, and rare, unusual plants.

Reading comprehension

1   **Choose the correct answer.**

1   The number of people who took part in the competition was:
   a 14   b 25   c over 20 million

2   Hampton Court is a:
   a prehistoric monument   b palace and grounds   c mountain

3   John Vanburgh:
   a organised the competition   b climbed Ben Nevis   c designed Castle Howard

4   Ben Nevis is:
   a 79m high   b 1,344m high   c 5,500m high

5   Castle Howard is in:
   a Yorkshire   b The Lake District   c Greater London

6   Wastwater is surrounded by:
   a a maze   b mountains   c gardens and a lake

7   The Giant's Causeway is made of:
   a Welsh stone   b Bluestone   c basalt

2   **Choose the correct meaning of each phrase.**

1   overwhelming response   a huge reaction   b small reaction
2   make an attempt   a look at   b try
3   remains a mystery   a is known   b is not known

3   **Discuss your answers.**

1   Why do you think Hampton Court 'is one of the city's most popular attractions'?
2   Why do you think it is 'puzzling' that stones were carried over a 'colossal distance' to Stonehenge?
3   Why do you think Castle Howard is a 'popular setting' for film and TV programmes?
4   Why do you think Ben Nevis was given that name?

Vocabulary check

Find these words in the article. Check any you are not sure of in your dictionary.

located (vb)   ascent (n)   majestic (adj)
prehistoric (adj)   attractions (n)   maze (n)
remodelled (vb)   grounds (n)   situated (vb)
fatalities (n)   residence (n)   summit (n)
private (adj)   hectares (n)   monument (n)

Your views

● Why do you think people were so interested in the competition?
● Which of the Wonders of the United Kingdom would you be most interested in visiting? Explain your reasons.
● If you had to choose one place in your country to be a 'Wonder', which would it be? Explain your reasons.

Looking at language

A Dictionary work
Words with two or more meanings 3

- Some words have **two or more meanings** for the **same part of speech** and **other meanings** for a **different part of speech**.
- Dictionaries sometimes give the various meanings for the same part of speech in the form of word boxes.

> **number¹** /ˈnʌmbə/ *noun*
> **1** amount   **4** quantity
> **2** position   **5** in language
> **3** telephone number

- The words in the word box will appear as entries to give you more information.

> 1 [C] **Maths** – a sign or word that represents an amount or quantity

> **number²** /ˈnʌmbə/ *verb* [T] **1** to give a number to something **2** to consist of a particular quantity of people or things

1 **Use a dictionary. How many meanings are there for each noun?**

1 leg   2 heart   3 hour   4 life

2 **Use a dictionary. Which of these words can be used as: a noun and verb? b noun and adjective?**

1 load   2 mass   3 heat
4 line   5 front   6 move

B Spelling
-ary / -ery / -ory

- The endings *-ary*, *-ery* and *-ory* can be easily confused. Always check in a dictionary.
  '... one of the United Kingdom's most **extraordinary** *attractions'*
  '... what other uses it had remain a **mystery**'

1 **Complete each adjective with -ary, -ery or -ory.**

1 compuls_____   2 silv_____   3 prim_____
4 rubb_____   5 explanat_____   6 solit_____
7 wat_____   8 second_____   9 advis_____
10 imagin_____   11 satisfact_____ 12 fi_____

2 **Look up the words *stationary* and *stationery* in a dictionary. Write a sentence for each word to show you understand the difference in meaning.**

C Language development
Order of subordinate clauses

- In Unit 6, you looked at complex sentences with more than one subordinate clause.
- Subordinate clauses often come after the main clause.
  There are about 40,000 basalt columns, **resulting from an ancient volcanic eruption.**
- A subordinate clause can come in the middle of a sentence.

1 **Find and underline the subordinate clause in this sentence.**

This majestic peak, standing at 1,344m, is the highest point in Great Britain.

- A subordinate clause can come before the main clause.

2 **Find and underline the subordinate clause in this sentence.**

Situated in the Lake District National Park, Wastwater holds many national records.

- In descriptive writing, both non-fiction and fiction, more than one subordinate clause may often come before the main clause.

3 **Find and underline the two subordinate clauses in this sentence.**

Built as a manor house in the 11th century and remodelled as a palace by Henry VIII, many say that it was the King's favourite residence.

To understand a sentence beginning with two or more clauses, find the main clause, then re-read.

Word building: prefix over-

- *over-* can be added to verbs, nouns, adjectives and adverbs.
- As a prefix, it has several meanings:
  too much, e.g. *overheat, overdue*
  outer, extra, e.g. *overcoat, overtime*
  above, across, e.g. *overhang, overland*
  a lot, e.g. *overjoyed, overwhelmed*

4 **Write the prefix for these words. Read them. Check any that are new in a dictionary. Discuss which meaning of *over-* each word has.**

1 _____grown   2 _____crowded   3 _____all
4 _____seas   5 _____come   6 _____look

Grammar

1 Read.

Stonehenge stands on a high plain in the southwest of England. It is a well-known ancient monument but much of its history remains a mystery. We know that 5,000 years ago it **was being used** as a burial site. Some historians suggest that it was a temple to the sun. Others believe that it was a giant calendar.

Thousands of tourists visit Stonehenge every year. This causes traffic jams on the roads around the monument and the small visitors centre near the stones becomes too crowded. Because of this, plans **are being drawn** up to provide a new visitors centre 2.5km from the stones. The new centre **is being designed** with cafés, shops, educational facilities and a large car park.

2 Cover the text. Read the statements. Write *T* (true) or *F* (false).

1 Stonehenge is situated in the northwest of England. _____
2 We do not know everything about its history. _____
3 We know that 5,000 years ago it was being used as a temple. _____
4 The visitors' centre is too small. _____
5 A new visitors' centre is being planned closer to the stones. _____
6 The new centre is being designed without cafés and shops. _____

Now correct the false statements.

3

Present continuous passive

We use this for actions which are happening now:
*The votes **are being counted**.*
*A new palace **is being built**.*
When you want to say who (or what) is doing the action, use **by**:
*John's portrait **is being painted by** a famous artist.*
*Look! The trees **are being blown down by** the storm.*

Change these sentences. Use the passive.

1 Someone is driving the car too fast.
   The car is being driven too fast.
2 They are renovating the palace.
3 They are drawing up plans.
4 Some people are making wild promises.
5 Some people are breaking the law.
6 Someone is organising a party.
7 They are putting up decorations.

4

Past continuous passive

We use this for actions which were happening at a particular time in the past:
*At midday the tourists **were being shown** the gardens.*
We also use this for actions which were interrupted by a sudden, shorter action:
*When Joe arrived home, dinner **was being cooked**.*
*While the play **was being performed**, a fire broke out in the theatre.*
When you want to say who (or what) was doing the action, use **by**:
*The car **was being driven by** a little old lady.*

Change these sentences. Use the passive.

1 At midnight someone was playing loud music.
   At midnight loud music was being played.
2 People were singing songs.
3 Some people were telling jokes.
4 Two hundred years ago people were farming this land.
5 They were growing wheat and cotton.
6 Someone was ringing a bell.

5 Ask and answer in pairs.

1 Who is organising the competition? (a magazine)
   The competition is being organised by a magazine.
2 Who is judging the entries? (a team of experts)
3 Who is choosing the winner? (a university professor)
4 Who is presenting the prizes? (a celebrity)
5 What was damaging the crops? (insects)
6 Who was buying this product? (teenage girls)

1 Listen and read. (2.10)

Ross: Holly is so **upset about** losing our work. She's **furious with** herself.
Laura: I know. She texted me in a panic. Poor Holly!
Ross: Do you think you can help? You're so **good at** IT.
Laura: Ross, there's no problem. I've got the whole project on my laptop.
Ross: Are you sure?
Laura: Of course, silly! I always make copies of everything.
Ross: Phew! What a relief!
Laura: And here's some more good news. I'm back on the project!
Ross: Really? How come?
Laura: Well, I had to tell Professor Brown that I couldn't carry on and he phoned up Mum and Dad and talked them round.
Ross: Amazing!
Laura: I'm **so grateful to** him! I was getting **fed up with** all the arguments.
Ross: I bet.
Laura: So tell me what's been going on. What are the other teams up to?
Ross: Well, the science team …
Laura: Usha in India and Ali in Jordan …
Ross: That's right. They're doing a feature on healthy eating and young people's eating habits.
Laura: I wonder if theirs are **different from** ours.
Ross: We'll find out. They've prepared a questionnaire.
Laura: Excellent!

2 Answer these questions.

1 Why is Holly furious with herself?
2 Why has Ross asked Laura for help?
3 Can Laura help? How?
4 What is Laura's good news?
5 Why is Laura grateful to Professor Brown?
6 What was she getting fed up with?
7 Why have Usha and Ali been in touch?
8 What have they prepared?

3 Complete these sentences using the prepositions in the box.

to   of   about   on   with

1 Holly is angry _____ herself.
2 Laura is tired _____ arguing with her parents.
3 Her parents are concerned _____ her schoolwork.
4 Jack is a little short _____ money.
5 His opinions are similar _____ hers.
6 The team is full _____ confidence.
7 They are proud _____ their achievements.
8 Laura is very keen _____ IT.

4 Find the prepositions which follow these adjectives in the dialogue. Make up your own sentences using these adjectives and prepositions.

1 upset _____ 2 furious _____
3 good _____ 4 grateful _____
5 fed up _____ 6 different _____

5 Talk about these questions in pairs.

1 What school subjects are you good at?
2 What sports are you keen on?
3 What other activities are you interested in?
4 Are you worried about anything?
5 What is your town famous for?

Remember!
Adjectives + prepositions
There are no rules!
*New York is **famous for** its skyscrapers.*
*Joe is **ashamed of** his behaviour.*
*Ellie is very **keen on** sport.*
*Laura is **interested in** films.*
*I've always been **bad at** maths.*

Grammar extra p129

> Magazines often include articles that give you information about things happening in other parts of the world. Unlike encyclopaedias, magazine articles are read in leisure time and, as well as being informative, must look attractive and inviting for the reader.

Features of magazine articles

▶ **Headline**

The **headline** is very important because it must catch the reader's eye and make them want to read on.

> **ACTIVITY**
> What is the **headline** of this article?
> Would the headline make you want to read the article? Why? / Why not?

▶ **Opening paragraph**

The headline has made the reader want to read the article. The **opening paragraph** must keep the reader interested and let them know what the article is about, i.e.

1 the competition   2 how it was organised

▶ **Tenses**

Some magazine articles are written about something that is in existence now so they are written in **present tenses**, e.g. 'The palace **is** surrounded by a breathtaking estate'

They can also give you historical information written in **past tenses**. e.g. '... it **was** begun about 5,500 years ago ...'

> **ACTIVITY**
> Find three more examples of **present tenses** and **past tenses** in the article. When would an article use **future tenses**? Find one example of the **future tense** in this article.

▶ **Detailed information**

The writers of magazine articles have to do their research thoroughly and give the reader lots of **detailed information**. The writer says:

> The name Ben Nevis translates as 'the mountain with its head in the clouds'.

NOT It's name has something to do with clouds.

> Situated on Salisbury Plain in the county of Wiltshire ...

NOT Somewhere in the United Kingdom.

> **ACTIVITY**
> Find three more pieces of **detailed information** in the article.

▶ **Sub-headings**

To help the reader understand the information in the article, the writer has used **sub-headings**.

> **ACTIVITY**
> How many **sub-headings** are in the article? In what way are they helpful to the reader?

▶ **Illustration**

Magazine articles must also be **attractive to look at**.
They can include maps, diagrams, photographs and drawings.

> **ACTIVITY**
> How is the article **illustrated**?
> Do you find it **attractive** to look at? Why? / Why not?

Writing together

> There are Seven Wonders of the Ancient World. Below is information about three of them. As a class, use the information to write three sections of a magazine article about the Seven Wonders.

The Colossus of Rhodes
Rhodes = Mediterranean Island
Attacked in 305 by Demetrius
Demetrius defeated
People of Rhodes built triumphal statue
Sculptor = Chares of Lindos
Took 12 years to complete
Base = white marble / framework = stone and iron / covered in bronze
33m high
226 BC – earthquake – statue in ruins

The Hanging Gardens of Babylon
Built by King Nebuchadnezzar
Reigned from 605–562 BC
Built to cheer up his wife, Amyitis
Amyitis from green, mountainous country – hated dry, flat landscape of Babylon
Hanging Gardens = artificial mountain with rooftop gardens – plants and huge trees
Said to be 122m wide / 122m long / 24.5m high

Pharos of Alexandria
Lighthouse
Situated in harbour of Alexandria
Alexandria – busiest port in ancient world / surrounded by dangerous sandbars
Lighthouse = 560m high
Architect = Sostratus / 17 years to build lantern at the top = giant bonfire / visible 56.5km out to sea
Ruined by earthquakes in 1303 & 1323

Remember!
• Think of an interesting **title** for the article to catch the reader's eye.
• Write a clear **opening paragraph** so the reader knows what the article is about.
• Think carefully about the **tenses** you need to use.
• Include all the **detailed information** from the notes.
• Use **sub-headings** for different parts of the article.
• Discuss what **illustrations** you will use and where you will place them.

WB p90

Conversation practice

1 Ross and Laura are talking. Look at the pictures and the words in the box. What do you think they are talking about?

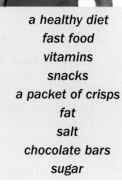

a healthy diet
fast food
vitamins
snacks
a packet of crisps
fat
salt
chocolate bars
sugar

2 [2.11] **Listen to Ross and Laura. Were you right?**

3 [2.11] **Listen again and note down all the foods that Ross eats. Whose diet is healthier, Ross's or Laura's?**

4 **Talk with your friends about your diets and what you like (and dislike) to eat.**

Start like this: *Do you think you eat a healthy diet?*

Listening comprehension

1 [2.12] **Look at the picture. What are Holly and Jack doing? Listen.**

2 [2.12] **Read the statements. Listen again and write T (true) or F (false).**

1 Holly always eats a good breakfast. ___
2 Jack's father says that breakfast is the most important meal of the day. ___
3 At break, Jack's snack is healthier than Holly's. ___
4 Holly has pizza for lunch at school. ___
5 At school Jack has a sandwich and a chocolate bar for lunch. ___
6 Jack sometimes eats cakes and biscuits. ___
7 Holly isn't fond of sweet things to eat. ___
8 Holly always has the same meal for dinner. ___
9 Jack is a vegetarian. ___
10 Jack's diet is healthier than Holly's. ___

Individual speaking

You are going to talk about your diet and say whether it is healthy or not. WB p91

Communications

Check-in

We have different ways of communicating in writing. Some of them are quick and informal. Others are more formal and take longer to write.

List all the methods you can think of for communicating information in writing.
Which do you use most often?
When do you use formal writing?
Think of two occasions when you would write a formal letter.

You are going to read some letters, emails and texts that were exchanged during the website project.

Reading

• Two teams **wanted some information** about the people of the Canadian First Nations.

Who are the First Nations people?

• The teams exchanged information between themselves.

How do you think they communicated with each other?

• Later, one team wrote two letters. One was **formal** and one was informal.

Which type of letter would you write to a person you do not know?

• These words are in the letters, emails and texts you are going to read.

    civilization admire authentic ancestors
       grateful freedom occasion

What do they mean? Check in a dictionary.

Looking at language

• Dictionary: **phrases**.
• Spelling: **words with *au / aw***.

Think of a word for each letter pattern.

• Language development: **conjunction *so***.

Grammar

• Practise **third conditional**.
• Practise ***wish* + past / past perfect + *would***.
• Practise **phrases with *pay***.

Writing

• Learn about the **features of formal letter writing**.
• Write a **formal letter** of enquiry.
• Write an **informal letter** to a friend.

Listening

• Holly and Jack's **discussion** about environmental problems.
• Team leaders giving their **personal views** on environmental issues.

Speaking

• Talk in a group about **environmental problems.**
• Tell the class about environmental concerns.

The First Nations

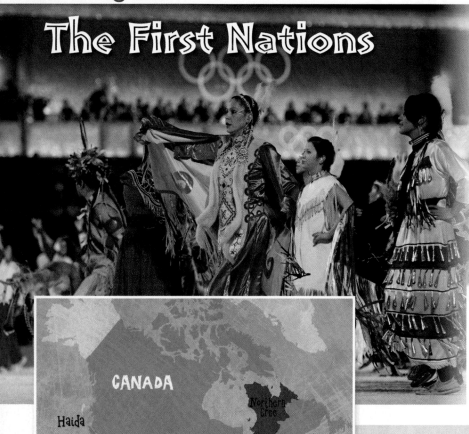

From: Robert
To: Brad
Cc: Sofia

Hi Brad,
The Kenyan and Brazilian teams have watched videos of the Canadian First Nations in the opening ceremony of the Winter Olympics™ in Vancouver, 2010, on the internet. Fantastic! We wish we'd been there! Can you recommend a website so we can find out more about the aboriginal peoples of Canada?
Robert

Canadian Museum
of Civilization.
www.civilization.ca
Gr8 site!
Brad

1093 Mountain Avenue
Thika
Kenya
18th January

Dr Paul Davis
Canadian Museum of Civilization
Quebec

Dear Dr Davis,

I am writing to thank you for sending us the information about your recent archaeological excavations in north-east Canada. We have read your blog on the website. Thank you, too, for sending us the email addresses of the school students who joined your team on the dig.

We have exchanged several emails with Carly Chego and Annie Benet. They told us how much they enjoyed excavating and how much they learned about the lives of their ancestors. They were particularly excited about the decorated pottery that was six thousand years old. If you had not replied to us, we would not have contacted them and we would not have made new friends across the ocean, so we are very grateful to you.

We have started to find out a lot more about the other First Nations of Canada. We had no idea there were so many different people speaking their own languages and with their own culture in modern Canada. Carly told us about her grandmother who does the most beautiful embroidery on animal skin and makes the same clothing that the Mi'kmaq people have been making for centuries. We have just started to find out about the Haida people on the north-west coast. We think the *Spirit of the Haida Gwaii* is a wonderful sculpture and we can understand why it is on the Canadian $20 note.

Thank you again for all your help. We would be grateful if you could let us know when you are starting your next dig. We would like to follow your blog live next time.

Yours sincerely,
Robert Githiga

Museum brill.
Check out Northern
Cree. Hand drum
competitions online.
Inspiring! *Sofia*

Expect
surprise
in post.
Carly

1093 Mountain Avenue
Thika
Kenya

25th February

Dear Mrs Chego,

Thank you very much for the beautiful quill box that you made and Carly sent to us. We've never seen anything like it. We have porcupines in Africa but we didn't know their quills could be used to decorate objects. I showed it to my aunt. She does traditional beadwork so she knows how long it takes to make things by hand. She was really interested in it and admired it very much.

Thanks for the photos of last year's pow wow and for telling us about your plans for this year. We wish we were coming! It looks like a wonderful occasion. We have traditional clothing in Kenya, too, but it's nothing like as spectacular.

We've all enjoyed finding out about the lives of First Nation people. My aunt says that it's important to keep traditional cultures alive. That's why she tells me old stories in Kikuyu, which is our language.

I'm sending you a photo of my aunt wearing traditional beadwork. I hope you like it.

Best wishes from,
Robert

From:	Carly
To:	Robert
Cc:	Sofia

Glad you liked the box, Robert. Quilling is an authentic Mi'kmaq craft. Grandma loves to make beautiful things and she insisted that I send it! My cousin Ellie was one of the shawl dancers for the Olympic opening. She wore a shawl that Grandma had made and embroidered – see attached photo. (I wish she'd make one for me but I can't dance!) I took it from a distance but you can still see the beautiful colours. We were so proud of Ellie and all the other First Nation people in the ceremony. It gave us freedom to show the world that our art and culture is alive and how much it means to us.
Let us know if we can do anything else for the website project. It sounds amazing. When will the site go live? Do you want some pow wow video clips? Recorded stories in Algonquin? Anything?
Carly

Reading comprehension

1   Answer these questions.

  1 How did the Kenyan and Brazilian teams watch the opening of the Winter Olympics™, 2010?

  2 What do the teams want to find out more about?

  3 Where does Brad tell them to look?

  4 What did Dr Paul Davis send to Robert?

  5 Who does Robert say they have exchanged several emails with?

  6 What had Carly and Annie done?

  7 How did they feel about the dig?

  8 What is the *Spirit of the Haida Gwaii*?

  9 What special event did Carly's grandmother send photos of?

 10 What special event was Ellie involved in?

2   Discuss these questions.

  1 Which communication has a formal ending and what is it?

  2 What is the ending for the informal letter?

  3 Which communication has just the name of the sender with no closing phrase?

  4 Which communication ends with no sender and no closing phrase?

  5 What does 'Gr8' mean? What does 'brill' stand for?

  6 What is missing at the start of Carly's email to Robert? Why has Carly left it out?

3   Find the phrases in the text. Underline the correct meaning, a or b.

1	nothing like as spectacular	a not as spectacular as	b much less spectacular than
2	check out	a have a look at	b leave out
3	by hand	a only using the hands	b using mostly one hand
4	let us know	a ask us	b tell us
5	go live	a move to another place	b become active

4   Discuss your answers to these questions.

 1 Do you think every continent has people with a traditional culture? If not, which ones do you think do not?

 2 What traditional cultures do you know of anywhere in the world?

 3 What traditional cultures can you think of in your own country?

Vocabulary check

Find these words in the text. Tick the words you know or can guess. Use a dictionary to look up any words that are new and check words you are not sure of.

> inspiring civilization post quill porcupine beadwork admire occasion authentic shawl
> video clip pow wow aboriginal excavation dig ancestors pottery grateful embroidery recent
> modern spirit craft freedom

Your views

- Which of these forms of communication do you use most often? Why?
- Which one do you use least? Why?
- Which one do you like to receive the most? Why?

A Dictionary work

Phrases

- Quite often there are **phrases** in English that are difficult to understand. These common phrases can be found in a dictionary. The **phrase** comes under the entry for the **first important word** in the phrase.

> **distance** /'dɪstəns/ *noun* the amount of space between two people or things
>
> PHRASES **from a distance** from a place that is not close; **into the distance** at a place that is very far from where you are; **keep your distance** avoid going near someone or something

I **Look at the entry for *life* in a dictionary.**

Find the PHRASES heading.
Read the definitions of these phrases and use them in sentences.

1 bring something to life 2 come to life
3 the time of your life

2 **Read each of these phrases. Decide which is the first important word in each phrase. Look in a dictionary and find the meaning of each phrase.**

1 as good as new   2 in living memory
3 fall into place   4 at great length
5 make a go of   6 not to mention

B Spelling

au / aw words

- The letters *au* and *aw* can sound the same in some words /ɔː/.
  *Quilling is an **authentic** Mi'kmaq craft.*
  *My cousin was one of the **shawl** dancers …*

I **Complete each word with *au* or *aw*.**

1 ___ ___ful   2 astron___ ___ t   3 str___ ___
4 h ___ ___k   5 f___ ___lt   6 cr___ ___l

2 **Match each of these words to the correct definition.**

drawl	1 to take something back
audible	2 loud enough for people to hear
withdraw	3 a slow way of speaking

C Language development

Conjunction: so

- The conjunction so can be used to introduce a subordinate clause.
- so can mean 'with the result that'.
  *She does traditional beadwork **so she knows how long it takes to make things by hand**.*

I **Underline the subordinate result clause in the sentence above.**

Complete this sentence with a clause that expresses the result of the first action.

Ben missed the bus to school so …

- The **result** clause must always come after the main clause.
- so can also mean 'in order that'. It tells you about the **purpose** of the first action.
  *Can you recommend a website **so we can find out more about the Canadian First Nations**?*

2 **Underline the subordinate clause in the sentence above.**

Complete this sentence with a clause that expresses the purpose of the first action.

Could you please open the window so …

- A subordinate clause of purpose can come before the main clause.
  ***So** he could reach the shelf, Ben stood on a chair.*

3 **Underline the subordinate clause in the sentence above.**

Re-write the sentence with the main clause coming first.

Decide whether these sentences show purpose or result. Write *P* or *R*.

1 We got to the cinema late so we missed the beginning of the film. ___
2 Grandma decided to get new glasses so she could read better. ___
3 The scientists did the experiment again so they could check their results. ___
4 Peter was feeling very ill when he did the exam so he did quite badly. ___

Grammar

1 Read.

Robert wants to know more about the aboriginal peoples of Canada. He watched some videos of the opening ceremony of the Winter Olympics™ in Vancouver in 2010. He also went on the internet and found some amazing pictures of dancers and musicians at pow wows.

If I had not watched the opening ceremony, I **would not have known** about the Canadian First Nations. **If I had not gone** on the internet, I **would not have** found the pictures.

Robert sent a letter to Dr Paul Davis at the Museum of Civilization in Quebec. Dr Davis replied to Robert and sent him information about the museum's archaeological excavations in north-east Canada. He also sent Robert the email addresses of two of the students who had worked on the dig. Robert got in touch with them. Carly and Annie sent Robert lots of interesting information about the First Nations in the present and the past.

If Dr Davis had not replied, I would not have got in touch with Carly and Annie. **I would have found out** much less about the First Nations **if Carly and Annie had not taken** an interest in the website project.

2 Answer these questions.

1 What did Robert watch? Why?
2 If he had not watched it, what would have happened?
3 What did Robert find on the internet?
4 If he had not gone on the internet, what would have happened?
5 Did Dr Davis reply to Robert's letter?
6 If Dr Davis had not replied to Robert, what would have happened?

3 Find the right endings. Write the letters.

1 Robert would not have known about the First Nations …
2 He would not have found the pictures of pow wows …
3 If Dr Davis had not sent the students' email addresses, …
4 If Robert had not got in touch with Annie and Carly, …

a Robert would not have got in touch with them.
b if he had not gone on the internet.
c he would not have made friends with them.
d if he had not watched videos of the Opening Ceremony.

4 Complete these sentences with the verbs in brackets.

1 If Robert _____ not _____ in touch with Dr Davis, he _____ not _____ friends with Annie and Carly. (get, make)
2 If Hampton _____ not _____ the *Portrait* project, they _____ not _____ to New York. (win, go)
3 Joe _____ on time if he _____ not _____. (arrive, oversleep)
4 I _____ you if I _____ not _____ your number. (phone, lose)

Remember!

Third conditional

We use this when we are thinking about a conditional situation **in the past**.

Joe went to Paris. He saw the Eiffel Tower.
***If** he **had not gone** to Paris, he **would not have seen** the Eiffel Tower.*
Lucy did not win the competition so she did not get a prize.
***If** she **had won** the competition, she **would have got** a prize.*
Either the *if* clause or the main clause can appear first.
***If I had seen** Sally, I **would have spoken** to her.*
*I **would have spoken** to Sally **if I had seen** her.*

Website Project
Saturday 3pm
Important meeting!!

1 🎧 2.14 Listen and read.

Laura: Ok ... is all our work ready to send to Professor Brown?

Jack: When's the launch happening?

Ross: Next Saturday.

Holly: It's so exciting! I **wish it was** next Saturday now!

Laura: Where's your work on the rainforests, Holly?

Holly: On the memory stick, I hope.

Ross: Don't forget my piece about using water wisely.

Jack: When's the launch happening?

Ross: Next Saturday! I wish you'd pay attention, Jack!

Laura: Our work on pollution is really excellent, I think.

Holly: The interview with Brad's dad about the oil spill in Alaska is just great.

Jack: I **wish I'd done** something on noise pollution. That's a big problem, too.

Holly: You can do it after the launch. The website is going to grow all the time, remember.

Laura: We've got so much material! I can't believe it!

Ross: I think we can be really proud of ourselves.

2 Answer these questions.

1 Why is today's meeting important?

2 Holly says, "I wish it was next Saturday now!" Why?

3 Ross say, "I wish you'd pay attention, Jack!" Why?

4 Which environmental topics have the young people covered?

5 Did Jack do any work on noise pollution?

6 Why can they be proud of themselves?

3 Complete these sentences. Use *would* + a phrase from the box.

> pay attention   phone her   be quiet
> hurry up   help me   be more careful

1 I can't do this by myself. I wish you ...
I wish you would help me.

2 Those children are so noisy! I wish they ...

3 Grandma's feeling lonely. She wishes you ...

4 You're not listening to me. I wish you ...

5 Jack is so clumsy. I wish he ...

6 Annie's being very slow. I wish she ...

4 Make sentences as in the example. Use *wish* + past simple or past continuous.

1 Annie doesn't like her curly hair.
She wishes it was straight. Or: She wishes it wasn't curly.

2 Billy doesn't have a pet.

3 I don't like this wet weather.

4 Susi can't play the piano very well.

5 Joe thinks his exams are always too hard.

6 The boys are losing their match.

5 Make sentences as in the example. Use *wish* + past perfect.

1 Billy failed his last exam.
He wishes he had passed. Or: He wishes he had revised more.

2 Sally didn't buy that CD.

3 We didn't go to the last Olympic Games™.

4 Joe was late for school this morning.

5 I got really wet walking home yesterday.

6 The girls lost their basketball game.

Remember!

Constructions with *wish*

- When we are thinking about a future situation, we use *wish* + *would* + verb.
  *It's my birthday next month. I **wish** my parents **would buy** me a guitar.*

- When we are talking about the present, we use *wish* + past tense.
  *Joe can't swim. He **wishes** he **could** swim.*
  *It's cloudy. I **wish** the sun **was** shining.*

- When we are talking about the past, we use *wish* + past perfect.
  *I didn't see that film. I **wish** I **had seen** it.*

Find examples of constructions with *wish* in the dialogue.

> *Grammar extra p130*

Writing

Features of formal letter writing

Formal letters are sent to people the writer does not know personally. Examples of formal letters are: job applications, requesting information, making a complaint, etc.

▶ **Layout**

The greeting:

a Dear Sir or Madam – used when you do not know the name of the person you are writing to.

b Dear [name] – in formal letters it is usual to address the person using their title and name, e.g. Mr Hurst / Professor Brown / Mrs Carter. If you are writing to a woman and do not know if she is married or not used the title Ms.

Your address: top right-hand corner of the first page

The address of the person you are writing to [the recipient]: Leave a line under the date. Go across to the left-hand side. Write the recipient's address.

1093 Mountain Avenue
Thika
Kenya
18th January

The date

Dr Paul Davis
Canadian Museum of Civilization
Quebec
Dear Dr Davis,

I am writing to thank you for sending us the information about your recent archaeological excavations in north-east Canada. We have read your blog on the website. Thank you, too, for sending us the email addresses of the school students who joined your team on the dig.

We have exchanged several emails with Carly Chego and Annie Benet. They told us how much they enjoyed excavating and how much they learned about the lives of their ancestors. They were particularly excited about the decorated pottery that was six thousand years old. If you had not replied to us, we would not have contacted them and we would not have made new friends across the ocean so we are very grateful to you.

The body of the letter: block paragraphed – leave a line between each paragraph and DO NOT indent.

We have started to find out a lot more about the other First Nations of Canada. We had no idea there were so many different people speaking their own languages and with their own culture in modern Canada. Carly told us about her grandmother who does the most beautiful embroidery on animal skin and makes the same clothing that the Mi'kmaq people have been making for centuries. We have just started to find out about the Haida people on the north-west coast. We think the *Spirit of the Haida Gwaii* is a wonderful sculpture and we can understand why it is on the Canadian $20 note.

Thank you again for all your help. We would be grateful if you could you let us know when you are starting your next dig. We would like to follow your blog live next time.

Yours sincerely,

Robert Githiga

The ending:

a 'Yours faithfully' if you do not know the person's name.

b 'Yours sincerely' if you know the person's name.

Your signature: sign the letter and then print your name in capitals. Put your title (Miss, Mr, etc.) in brackets after your printed name.

Content

The first paragraph is short and clearly states the **purpose** of the letter. The reader needs to know what sort of letter it is. Are you writing to complain, ask for a refund, express interest, apologise, express thanks, seek information?

ACTIVITY What is the **purpose** of Robert Githiga's letter?

The body of the letter should explain in detail **why you have written**, giving any relevant information the recipient needs.

ACTIVITY What is Robert Githiga saying in **the body of the letter**?

The final paragraph should make it clear **what action you require**. Do you want a reply, more information, do you want the recipient to do something?

ACTIVITY What **action** does Robert Githiga want Paul Davis to take?

Writing together

Bill Reid was the sculptor who created the *Spirit of the Haida Gwaii*. As a class, you are going to write a formal letter to The Bill Reid Foundation asking for information about the artist and his work.

Things to think about.

The address

Bill Reid Foundation, 639 Hornby Street, Vancouver, BC Canada, V6C 2GS

The first paragraph

Briefly state why you are writing.

The body of the letter

Organise what you want to know in paragraphs:

His life
- When was he born / died?
- Who were his parents?
- How did he become a sculptor?

His work:
- How many models did he make in his lifetime?
- How was the *Black Canoe* made?
- How big and how heavy is it?
- What is the *Jade Canoe*?

The final paragraph

- Decide how you would like to get this information.
- Do you want it in a letter?
- Do you want a book or website recommended?
- You also want to know if you can see any of his works outside of Canada.
- Remember to thank the recipient for their time.

Write your formal letter using the suggestions above.

Remember!
- Look carefully at page 104 for the **layout** of your letter.
- Don't just write a list of questions.
- **Begin** and **end** the letter correctly.

WB p99

Conversation practice

1 Holly and Jack are talking. Look at the pictures and the words
in the box. What do you think they are talking about?

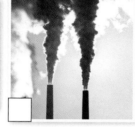

> pollution   traffic jams   fumes   oil spill   destruction
> global warming   habitats   endangered species
> extinct   recycling   recycle

2 [2.15] Listen to Holly and Jack. Were you right?

3 [2.15] Listen again. In what order do Holly and Jack speak about the environmental problems above?
Number the pictures from 1–6 in the correct order.

4 Talk with your friends about some of the world's environmental problems.

Start like this: *What do you think the most important environmental problems are?*

Listening comprehension

1 [2.16] Some of the team leaders are talking about environmental problems which are important to them.
Listen and write their concerns below each person. Sometimes they have more than one concern.

> water conservation   water pollution   air pollution   global warming   endangered species

Usha

Sergei

Tippi

Ali

Brad

_____   _____   _____   _____   _____

_____   _____   _____   _____   _____

2 [2.16] Read these questions. Listen again and answer the questions.

1 According to Usha, what can water pollution cause?
2 According to Sergei, how could the air quality in big cities be improved?
3 According to Tippi, how is Bangkok similar to Moscow?
4 According to Ali, why does his country have a problem with providing enough water?
5 According to Brad, what effect is global warming having on his country?

Individual speaking

You are going to talk about environmental concerns in your own country.

WB p100

I'm going to talk about ...

11

Check-in

Different people make presentations as part of their work. A lecture is a kind of presentation and so is a commentary made by a tour guide.

Have you ever listened to a presentation? What was it about?
How many times have you made a presentation to your class?
What do you think is the most difficult part of making a presentation?

You are going to read advice about giving a class presentation.

Reading

- The **advice** tells you what to do at the beginning and how to choose your topic if you need to.

What topic would you choose to make a presentation about?

- It **gives guidance** on doing your research, organising your notes and making your talk interesting.
- It gives you some last-minute tips.

What is a tip?

- These words are in the advice you are going to read.
  privacy   duration   tedious   ensure   relevant

What do they mean? Check in a dictionary.

Looking at language

- Dictionary: **phrasal verbs**.
- Spelling: **silent _u_**.
- Language development: **compound adverbs; suffix _-dom_**.

Grammar

- Learn the **future continuous tense**.
- Practise **question tags**.
- Practise **phrasal verbs with _hand_**.

Writing

- Learn about the **features of preparing for a class presentation**.
- Writing notes for a class presentation.
- Preparing a class presentation.

Listening

- Holly and Jack's **conversation** about computers.
- Laura's **presentation** on the website project.

Speaking

- Talk in a group about **computers**.
- Tell the class about creating a student website for your school.

Giving a class presentation

You've probably had to stand up and talk to your class, haven't you? Giving a presentation can be a nerve-wracking experience. You can, however, make life easier for yourself by preparing thoroughly and being familiar with the material by practising in the privacy of your own room.
Here's how to go about it.

At the beginning

Are you choosing your own topic or is one being given to you?

Choosing your own topic:
Although you have been given the freedom to choose your own topic, think very carefully. Do not select something you know nothing about. Choose something you have some knowledge of, are interested in and that your audience will be interested in.

Given a topic:
Ensure you know exactly what is required. Are there certain aspects that you should concentrate on?

Find out the duration of the presentation.

Is this a group presentation or an individual one?

We must work as a group, mustn't we?

Group presentation:
If you will be working in a group, decide what aspect of the topic you are presenting and how long you have to speak.

Research

Make sure that you:
- use several sources for the information you need. Just looking at one book or website is not a good idea. This will not give you a broad range of information, will it?
- make detailed notes on the information you find – your audience will know if you are vague and unprepared.
- group your notes under different aspects of the topic you are presenting. This will help you to quickly organise the final text.

Organising the text

Review the notes you have made under different headings.
Decide in what order you will be presenting the information.

↓

If you find it helpful, write down your text in full first.

You should then condense the information onto small cards.

Write key words and use different colours to jog your memory.

You would find it tedious just listening to someone read, wouldn't you? So will the audience!

↓

Making your presentation interesting

You need to engage the audience's interest throughout your presentation.

Just standing and talking can be quite boring so think about:

• using technology. You may decide to use a whiteboard, a projector, etc. but make sure you have practised with the technology beforehand. Don't let the first time you use it be when you are actually giving your talk!

• using visual aids. As well as giving your audience pictures, diagrams, etc. to look at, you may be able to hand around relevant objects that will make your presentation more interesting.

↓

Last-minute tips

Make sure you:

• are there before your audience

• have checked any equipment you are using

• sorted your note cards into the correct order

• have a glass of water on the table – talking is thirsty work!

↓

And remember ...

• Don't forget to look up at your audience. They don't want to be staring at the top of your head as you read your notes.

• Speak slowly and clearly. You will be giving an interesting presentation but it is not much use if no one can hear you.

• Leave time at the end for questions. If you do not know a particular answer, don't guess! Someone else in the room may come to your rescue, or you can make a note of the question and promise to find out the answer as soon as possible.

Reading comprehension

1   Answer these questions.

1   If you are choosing your own topic to talk about:
   a   what **should** you do?
   b   what **shouldn't** you do?
2   How many sources should you use for your information? Why?
3   What should you do with the information you find?
4   Why is it useful to include headings in your notes?
5   If you are using technology, what must you do?
6   When you are giving your presentation, how should you speak? Why?

2   Find the expressions in the text. Work out the correct meaning for each expression.

1   nerve-wracking
    a   pleasant and easy
    b   worrying

2   broad range of information
    a   a little information from one source
    b   lots of information from different sources

3   jog your memory
    a   help you remember
    b   help you forget

4   come to your rescue
    a   cause you to be embarrassed
    b   save you from embarrassment

3   Discuss your answers to these questions.

1   Why do you think it is important to know:
   a   if it is a group or individual presentation?
   b   the duration of the presentation?
2   Why do you think:
   a   'reading' the whole presentation **is not** a good idea?
   b   having 'relevant objects' to hand round **is** a good idea?
3   Why do you think you should be 'there before your audience'?
4   Why do you think you shouldn't 'guess' the answer to a question from the audience?

Vocabulary check

Find these words in the text. Check any you are not sure of in a dictionary.

> nerve-wracking   thoroughly   privacy   select   ensure   required   aspect   duration
> several   review   tedious   condense   beforehand   relevant

Write these headings in your book. Put each of the words from Activity 3 under the correct heading as they are used in the text.

<u>noun</u>   <u>adjective</u>   <u>verb</u>   <u>adverb</u>

Your views

- Have you ever given a presentation? How did you feel before, during and after the presentation?
- Would you prefer to give a group presentation or an individual one? Explain your reasons.
- Do you find the advice in the text helpful or unhelpful? Explain your reasons.

A Dictionary work

Phrasal verbs

- **Phrasal verbs** consist of a **root verb** such as *go*, *put*, *set*, etc. and an **adverb** or **preposition** such as *way*, *on*, *out*, etc. The phrasal verb comes under the entry for the verb.

> **go** /gəʊ/ *verb* to move or travel to a place
>
> PHRASAL VERB **go about something** to start dealing with a problem, situation or job in a particular way

1 **Look at the entry for *go* in a dictionary.**

Find the PHRASAL VERB heading.

Read the definition of these phrasal verbs and use them in sentences of your own.

> go back   go by   go ahead   go out

2 **Find the definition of the phrasal verb *write down* in the reading passage. Use these phrasal verbs in sentences of your own.**

> write back   write in   write off

B Spelling

Silent *u*

- Some words in English have a **silent *u***.
  … your audience will know if you are **vague** *…*
  … don't **guess**.

1 **Match each word with the correct definition.**

> *guitar   guilty   guide   disguise   tongue*

1 long, soft piece of flesh in the mouth
2 not innocent
3 something that someone wears so they will not be recognised.
4 a stringed musical instrument
5 to show someone where to go by going with them

C Language development

Compound adverbs

- Some adverbs are made of two or more words put together.
  You can, **however**, *make life easier for yourself by preparing thoroughly and being familiar with the material by practising in the privacy of your own room.*
  Thorough preparation will make your talk less stressful for you and, **moreover**, *you will give a better talk.*

1 **Match these phrases to the compound adverbs.**

in addition _____   in spite of that _____

Read these sentences.

Practice takes time but, **nevertheless**, *it is worth doing.*
Visual aids will help you explain things and, **furthermore**, *they make your talk more interesting.*

2 **These compound adverbs are synonyms of *however* and *furthermore*. Match them.**

nevertheless _____
furthermore _____

> *Always use a dictionary to check meanings if you are not sure.*

- *however* can also mean *no matter how*.
  Make sure you go through your talk several times, **however** *long it takes.*
- *however* can also mean *in whatever way*.
  Make your talk interesting **however** *you like.*
- In conversation, *however* can mean *in what way*?
  Look at that broken window! **However** *did that happen?*

Word building: suffix *-dom*

- A few nouns in English end in *-dom*.
  Although you have been given the **freedom** *to choose your own topic, think very carefully.*

3 **Complete these words. Check their meanings if necessary.**

1 bore_____   2 wis_____   3 king_____

Use each word in a sentence of your own.

Grammar

1 Read.

I'm having a terrible weekend. At school on Monday morning I've got to give a presentation and I'm dreading it. I'm very shy so I hate doing anything like this. **I'll be standing** there at the front of the class and everybody **will be looking** at me. What a nightmare!

Dad popped his head round my door just now. "Annie, **will you be doing** schoolwork all weekend?" he asked. "We're going to the mall tomorrow. Can't you come with us?"

"I'd love to, Dad, but I'm too busy."

I've done a lot of research, I've made notes and I've practised what I'm going to say in front of the mirror but I'm still feeling nervous. I know that on Monday morning I'**ll be feeling** sick and I'**ll be shaking** like a leaf. I wish I had more confidence!

Anyway, I'**ll be phoning** Jenny later. She's my best friend and we always have a chat in the evening. She'll cheer me up.

2 Cover the text and say if the following sentences are true or false. Check your answers. Correct the false statements.

1 Annie has got to give a presentation tomorrow.
2 She is looking forward to giving her presentation.
3 She'll be preparing her presentation all weekend.
4 She'll be feeling fine on Monday morning.
5 She'll be phoning her grandma later.

3 Complete the sentences with the verbs in the box. Use the future continuous.

get up   wait   give   sleep   fly   go

1 At nine o'clock on Monday morning Annie _____ her presentation.
2 This time next week Fred and his family _____ first class to Australia.
3 When you get to the airport, we _____ for you.
4 John's not well but tomorrow he _____ to work as usual.
5 I don't want to miss my flight so I _____ at five in the morning.
6 If you phone Uncle Jim in the middle of the night, he _____.

4 Make polite questions asking for information. Use the future continuous.

1 Miss Jones – teach – us – tomorrow?
   Will Miss Jones be teaching us tomorrow?
2 you – give – your presentation – this week?
3 your brother – go – university – October?
4 the president – pay – a visit – our town?
5 he – arrive – morning or afternoon?
6 he and his wife – come – our school?

Remember!
Future continuous

We use the future continuous:
- to talk about events which will be in progress at a particular time in the future.
  *Next year **my sister will be studying** at university.*
- to talk about things that we expect to happen in the normal course of events.
  I'll be seeing Jack at school tomorrow.
- to ask for information in a polite way.
  ***Will you be coming** to the party this evening?*

In all the examples above, *will be* + present participle can be replaced by *going to be* + present participle.
  *This time tomorrow **I'll be flying** to Paris.*
  *This time tomorrow **I'm going to be flying** to Paris.*

5 Read the text in Activity 1 again. Find examples of the three uses of the future continuous.

Sunday 10 am
Website launch!!!

1 🔊 Listen and read.

Holly: This is so exciting! I can't wait!

Jack: It'll come online at ten o'clock, **won't it**?

Ross: Yes. Just a few more minutes to go.

Laura: What time will it be in Russia? Will Sergei be able to see it?

Jack: It'll be one o'clock in the afternoon there, **won't it**?

Ross: Yes, I think so.

Holly: Brad won't be able to see it, **will he**? It'll be the middle of the night in Vancouver.

Jack: We should text him, **shouldn't we**, and wake him up.

Ross: He'll be awake, I'm sure. He wouldn't miss this for anything.

Holly: What's the time? Is it ten?

Laura: Yes, it is. I'm going to go online.

Jack: Come on! Hurry up! You haven't forgotten the web address, **have you**?

Laura: Of course not. OK. Wait a second and …

Holly: There it is! There's our website!

Jack: I can't believe it! It looks amazing!

Laura: The web designers have done a brilliant job, **haven't they**?

Ross: They certainly have. This is fantastic! Absolutely fantastic!

2 Answer these questions.

1 Is it morning or evening in Hampton?
2 What are Laura and her friends waiting for?
3 How are they feeling?
4 Why does Jack say that they should text Brad?
5 Why is Jack impatient?
6 What do they think of the website?

3 Remember!

Question tags with future tenses (simple and continuous)

*Professor Brown will be delighted, **won't he**?*
*Brad won't be sleeping, **will he**?*

Add the question tags.

1 Laura will put in the right web address, …
2 She won't make a mistake, …
3 All the teams will be watching, …
4 The website will be a huge success, …
5 You won't be disappointed, …
6 Brad won't miss the launch, …

4 Remember!

Question tags with the present perfect (simple and continuous)

*The teams have worked hard, **haven't they**?*
*Laura hasn't been neglecting her work, **has she**?*

Add the question tags.

1 You haven't seen the website yet, …
2 Laura has enjoyed working on the project, …
3 Jack's learned a lot about other countries, …
4 The project hasn't been a waste of time, …
5 They've been working hard for months, …
6 We haven't been working on the project, …

5 Remember!

Question tags with modal verbs

*Laura must put in the right web address, **mustn't she**?*
*We can't see the website yet, **can we**?*
*Jack should text Brad, **shouldn't he**?*
*Brad might be asleep, **mightn't he**?*

Use your own ideas to finish the sentences. Use question tags. Share your ideas with the rest of the class.

1 We mustn't …
2 You shouldn't …
3 I can …
4 Our teacher might …
5 You must …
6 We can't …
7 I should …
8 We ought to …

> Grammar extra p130

Writing

Features of preparing for a class presentation

> Thorough preparation for a class presentation is very important. Many of the features are exactly the same as if you were researching a non-fiction topic and producing a piece of written work to be marked. But there are some differences that you need to learn about.

▶ **Research to final copy**

You have learned about the stages from **research** to the **final copy** in *English World* 7. Here is a reminder.

> **Stage 1 – Research:** Use books, magazines and the web.
>
> ↓
>
> **Stage 2 – Making notes:** Write down important words and phrases.
>
> ↓
>
> **Stage 3 – Ordering your notes:** Group information under different headings.
>
> ↓
>
> **Stage 4 – The first draft:** Use your notes to write the first draft.
>
> ↓
>
> **Stage 5 – Proofreading:** Correct spelling, grammar and punctuation.
>
> ↓
>
> **Stage 6 – Final copy:** Give your work a title and copy it out neatly.

▶ **The differences**

Stages 1–3 are the same whether you are preparing a piece of written work or a **class talk**. You may feel more comfortable if you have also included Stage 4 – The first draft, but if you can just work from your notes, it will be quicker.

▶ **Key words and phrases**

The notes you need for a class talk are **key words and phrases** that you can then put into complete sentences as you speak. Here are some ways of doing this.

- Do not use unnecessary words. Do not write four words if one will do!

  in this day and age = now

> **ACTIVITY**
>
> **Shorten** these phrases.
> 1 in the not too distant future (2 words)
> 2 people who make their living by fishing (1 word)
> 3 at 12 o'clock in the night (1 word)

- Sentences are not required in notes.

What you write	What you say
Bangkok – Grand Palace – built 1782	The Grand Palace in Bangkok was built in 1782.

> **ACTIVITY**
>
> **Expand** each line of notes into **a complete sentence**.
> 1 Metropolitan Museum of Art – opened 1870 – world's largest
> 2 text messaging – poor spelling
> 3 class presentation – speak – clearly

> **ACTIVITY**
>
> Write the **key words and phrases** from these sentences.
> 1 Times Square is a busy, noisy place at all hours of the day and night.
> 2 Professor Brown told the students that they were going to create a website.
> 3 Text messaging is a quick way to pass on information, ask and respond to questions and make arrangements.

Short forms

Here are a few tips to keep your notes as short as possible.
- Use numbers instead of writing in full.
  1, 2, 3, etc.   rather than   *One / First / Firstly; Two / Second / Secondly*, etc.
- Use symbols instead of words.
  & = and   % = per cent   # = number
- Use arrows to connect points.
  Brasilia ⟶ planned for 500,000 ⟶ now 2 million
- Use abbreviations.
  NE = north-east   mm = millimetre   gov = government $ = dollar

Writing together

> **You are going to read a piece of information text and condense it into note form in preparation for a class presentation.**

Read the passage carefully.

The Cave Paintings of Solidade

In the village of Solidade in north-east Brazil, there has been a remarkable discovery. Some years ago, the villagers were about to destroy some limestone rocks. They wanted to make and sell whitewash made from the limestone. The rock face was four hundred square metres and on it were rock paintings that were between 2,000 and 7,000 years old.

The paintings were created by prehistoric Indian tribes and show parrots, cranes, macaws, lizards, frogs, turtles and plants.

Geologists were searching for oil in the area. What they discovered was these paintings. Eduardo Bagnoli, one of the geologists, persuaded firstly the villagers not to destroy the paintings, and secondly, his company to give 40,000 dollars to build a museum in the village.

Twenty-three local teenagers have been trained to act as guides. A tourist centre and souvenir shop have also been created. The villagers are now waiting for the tourists to come and be amazed at the spectacular paintings.

Make notes of all the important facts.
Condense your notes as much as possible.

> **Remember!**
> - Don't use **more** words than you have to.
> - Don't write in **complete sentences**.
> - Use **numbers**, **symbols**, **arrows** and **abbreviations**.

WB p110

Conversation practice

1 **Holly and Jack are talking. Look at the pictures and the words in the box. What do you think they are talking about?**

laptop   chat
send messages
website   fashion
projects   presentations
emails

2 **🎧2.19 Listen to Holly and Jack. Were you right?**

3 **🎧2.19 Listen again. In what order do Holly and Jack speak about some of the uses of computers? Number the computer screens from 1–7 in the correct order.**

4 **Talk with your friends about what you use computers for.**
   Start like this: *Have you got your own computer?*

Listening comprehension

1 **🎧2.20 Laura is going to give a presentation to her class. What topic will she choose? Listen. Were you right?**

2 **🎧2.20 Read these sentences. Listen again and circle the correct words.**

1 The teams first met **five / nine / nineteen** months ago.
2 **Some / All / None** of them have become close friends.
3 Laura is **happy / not happy / thrilled** with the website.
4 In the beginning **four / nine / thirty-six** students were working on the project.
5 Three hundred people contributed to the project **before / after** it went online.
6 **Many more / A few more / The same number** have since visited the website.
7 **Two thousand / Forty-five / Some** visitors have left messages.
8 Laura quotes messages from **Japanese / dissatisfied / enthusiastic** visitors.
9 There are **more / fewer** photos than messages.
10 The website will **get bigger / get smaller / stay the same size**.

Individual speaking

You are going to talk about creating a student website for your school.

WB p111

A new website

Check-in

Millions of websites are available on the internet.
People all over the world create them.

> *What are your favourite websites?*
> *What makes websites easy to use?*
> *What makes them difficult to use?*
> *What are your favourite features on a website?*

You are going to read parts of the home page of the young people's website.

Reading

- The **website** is called Global Youth Link.

> *Do you think that is a good name for the website?*

- The pages show the kind of material users can access.

> *What were the four subject areas that the teams of students were working on?*

- The home page has **links** to the four areas.

> *What other features would you expect to see on the website?*

- These words are used on the pages you are going to read.

> submit   catalogue   assemble   responsible
> encyclopaedia   expand   crucially

> *What do they mean? Check in a dictionary.*

Looking at language

- Dictionary: **synonyms**.
- Spelling: **tricky words**.
- Language development: **tones in writing; suffixes -age, -ship**.

> *Find a word ending with each suffix.*

Grammar

- Practise *either / or*; *neither / nor*; **past perfect passive**.
- Practise **adverbs of degree + adjective**.
- Practise **using *say* or *tell***.

Writing

- Learn about the **features of evaluative writing**.
- Write an evaluation of the Global Youth Link website.
- Write an evaluation of a real website.

Listening

- Ross and Laura's **discussion** of the home page.
- The team leaders' **personal views** by video link.

Speaking

- Talk in groups about the **website home page**.
- Tell the class about your own views of the website.

www.globalyouthlink.org

GLOBAL YOUTH LINK

| HOME | ART | SCIENCE | ENVIRONMENT |

The project

How it started
A Portrait of our town
Winning projects

New York
Diaries
Presentations
Reviews
Photo gallery

How to join in
Comment
Add to the website
Submit material to the
online archive and
catalogue

About us
The teams

Canada	Kenya
Brazil	India
Australia	Thailand
Russia	
UK	
Jordan	

Staff
Web manager
Giorgi Dolidze, Georgia
Co-ordinators
– international
Prof Brown, UK
Dr Naseer, Egypt
– National

Global Youth Link is launched!

A message from the website creators…

Welcome to the Global Youth Link website. We hope you enjoy looking at everything on the site and reading the pages.

It seems a long time since we all met in New York to start the project off. Back then, we didn't know each other and we didn't always know much about each other's countries, either. That's all changed!

Over the last year we've been constantly in touch by all possible means – from one-word texts to video conferences and from online social media to snail mail. Our task has been to find out young people's experiences in the fields of art, education, environment and science, their views about them and their hopes and expectations of them for the future.

In the process of assembling these, we've contacted hundreds of other young people. We've followed links and joined in blogs. We've set up online discussions and we've received hundreds of photos, video clips and sound recordings.

Each team has been responsible for one of the fields. Together we've discussed all the information we've received and we planned together how we would include it and present it on the website. If you click on one of the subject areas, you can explore all the material for that field.

You can respond to anything and you can add more content. This is only the beginning. Help us make it grow into an encyclopaedia of ideas, thoughts and information from young people worldwide!

Carrie Usha Robert Brad Tippi Ali
Sofia Sergei Laura Holly Dalia
Jack Hassan Ali Mona Ross Igor

Team members ☒
Ali
Dalia
Hassan
Mona

Dalia Baroud | personal message | profile   ☒

It's been hard work a lot of the time – well, all of the time, to tell the truth! I'm thrilled to have the friendship of people on every continent. They've expanded my world and given me new ideas. This has been a life-changing experience and I'm not the same person that I was when we started. I've learned so much about other people, and, crucially, about myself, too.

EDUCATION

Views

Everyone we contacted or who contacted us believes that education is important. We found out that getting a good education is not so easy for some people as it is for others. Where you live makes a big difference to your opportunities. In some places, the circumstances of your family and your parents' ability to pay can make a big difference, too. We received this message from a fifteen-year-old Kenyan girl who told us:

"Many children in Africa still cannot go to school. Either their parents are too poor to pay or there is no school for them to go to. This situation is neither just nor necessary. The right to education is a human right. That means it is for every child. Governments could do more for education but often they spend money on things that we don't need, like arms and huge government buildings. Education is more important than either of these."

Do you agree? Post your views here:

Write your view here

15 minutes ago
That's rubbish, Ani. We need teachers more than we need soldiers.
Greg, Canada

30 minutes ago
I don't agree that education is more important than defence. We need armies to keep us safe.
Ani, Georgia

35 minutes ago
I agree. It's very unfair that some children can't go to school.
Sarah, UK

Sports Russia

Canadian First Nation students campaign for a new school
Read more >>

- - - - - - - - - - - - - -

Thai students learn Geography from a helicopter
Read more>>

Santa Maria High School, Brazil City. Number of students 2000
Grades 7–11
Read more>>

Video catalogue
view by suject
view by length

Photo gallery
more>>

Sound tracks
poetry recital, Jordan
The creation of the world, Aboriginal myth in English and Tiwi, Australia
more>>

Reports

Recounts
Travelling to Amazonian school by canoe
more >>

School profiles
Canada	27
Brazil	20
Jordan	21
Russia	30
India	29
Kenya	16
Thailand	25
UK	32
Australia	35

Reading comprehension

1 Answer these questions.

The message:

1 Who is the message from?
2 What four fields have they worked on?
3 What have the teams received from other young people?
4 What two things can people accessing the site do?

The left bar:

5 How did the project start?
6 What aspects of the week in New York can you access?
7 How can you join in the project?
8 What information can you find out about the teams?

Education:

9 What does everyone say about education?
10 What two things can make a difference to your educational opportunities?
11 What does the girl say governments often spend money on instead of education?

The right bar:

12 What can you listen to that was recorded in Jordan?
13 What reports can you read?
14 Where is the school that appears under school profiles?

www.globalyouthlink.org

GLOBAL YOUTH LINK

HOME   ART   SCIENCE

The project
How it started
A Portrait of our town
Winning projects

New York
Diaries
Presentations
Reviews
Photo gallery

How to join in

Global Youth Link is launched!
A message from the website creators…
Welcome to the Global Youth Link website. We hope you enjoy looking [...]
site and reading the pages.
It seems a long time since we all met in New York to start the project of [...]
didn't know each other and we didn't always know much about each o[...]
either. That's all changed!
Over the last year we've been constantly in touch by all possible means[...]
texts to video conferences and from online social media to snail mail. [...]
find out young people's experiences in the fields of art, education, envi[...]
their views about them and their hopes and expectations of them for th[...]

2 Find these phrases in the text. Discuss what they mean then answer the questions.

video conference   social media   snail mail   human right

1 Which would you use to chat to your friends?
2 Which means something that is due to you as a person?
3 Which one involves letters and packages?
4 Which allows you to see and speak to several people in different places at the same time?

Think about the words you know. Look up the ones you don't.

3 Discuss your answers to these questions.

1 What do you like about the site? What do you not like?
2 What other general information about the project would you like to see on the website?
3 Did Dalia enjoy doing the project? How do you know?
4 Is it a good idea to have a *Views* section? Why? / Why not?
5 What view would you add to those that are already there?

Vocabulary check

Find these words in the text. Tick the words you know or can guess. Look up any new words in a dictionary.

left bar: submit   archive   catalogue
message: constantly   conference   expectation   assemble   responsible   content   encyclopaedia
personal message: friendship   expand   crucially
views: circumstances   opportunity   situation   just   ability   arms

---

Your views

● What comment would you make about the idea of the website project for young people?
● Which of the four fields would you want to explore first? Why?
● What views or ideas of your own could you add to the website?

A Dictionary work

Synonyms

- A feature of some dictionaries is **synonyms**. You may have used the same word lots of times, and you want to find other, more interesting words that mean the same.

famous /ˈfeɪməs/ *adjective* if someone or something is famous, a lot of people know their name or have heard about them; **famously** (adv.)

Build your vocabulary: words you can use instead of **famous**

- **eminent** – famous and respected for doing important work
- **legendary** – very famous and admired by many people
- **notorious / infamous** – famous for something bad
- **renowned** – famous for a special skill or achievement
- **well-known** – fairly famous

1 **Look up *cook* (v) in a dictionary. There are six other words you could use instead of *cook*. Rewrite this paragraph, using the word *cook* only once.**

*It was my turn to **cook** dinner. Earlier I had **cooked** the bread in the oven. I peeled and **cooked** the potatoes in water. I don't like to **cook** meat in a frying pan so I **cooked** it under the grill. I put a little oil on the vegetables and **cooked** them in the oven.*

2 **Write the simple word for each group of synonyms.**

1 chat   discuss   gossip   speak
2 chew   munch   nibble   gobble

B Spelling

Tricky words

English spelling can be very tricky for many reasons.

- silent letters, e.g. *buildings, listen, scissors*
- double letters, e.g. *immediate, necessary*
- words from other languages, e.g. *encyclopaedia, archaeology, rheumatism*
- suffixes, e.g. *discussion, investigation, pleasure*

1 **Correct the spelling mistakes.**

1 inocent   2 gitar   3 casle
4 solusion   5 choyce   6 meature

C Language development

Different tones in writing

The website shows
- a message from the teams
- a personal message
- comments about the views.
They vary in how formal or informal they are.

1 **Categorise these writing features as *F* (formal) or *I* (informal).**

1 short forms ___   2 incomplete sentences ___
3 full forms ___   4 exclamations ___
5 missing words ___   6 precise vocabulary ___
7 complete sentences ___   8 precise punctuation ___

Read these extracts. Order the extracts. Number the most formal 1 and the least formal 4. Use the writing features in Activity 1 to help you decide.

☐ *It's been hard work a lot of the time – well, all of the time, to tell the truth!*

☐ *We found out that getting a good education is not so easy for some people as it is for others.*

☐ *Rubbish, Ani!*

☐ *In the process of assembling these, we've contacted hundreds of other young people.*

Answer these questions.

1 Which section of the website is most formal?
2 Why do you think this style of writing was used for this section?
3 Which is the least formal?
4 Which sections are in between formal and informal?
5 Why do you think this style was chosen for these sections?

Word building: suffix *-age*

Some nouns end *-age*, e.g. mess**age**.

2 **Complete these words.**

1 lugg_____   2 cour_____

Word building: suffix *-ship*

A few nouns end in *-ship*, e.g. friend**ship**.

3 **Complete these words.**

1 hard_____   2 fellow_____

Grammar

1 Read.

Laura opened her laptop and typed in the web address. Immediately the Global Youth Link home page filled the screen.

"It looks amazing!" she thought.

The website **had been designed** by two young university students. They **had been helped** by a computer expert at the university, one of Professor Brown's colleagues. They had certainly done a fantastic job. It **had been put together** with young people in mind. The colours, the artwork, the photos, even the fonts **had been chosen** to appeal to young people.

The section entitled 'About us. The Teams.' caught Laura's eye. "Which team shall I look at first?" she wondered. "**Either** Australia **or** Russia, I think." She clicked on Australia and a list of names appeared. She clicked on the name 'Carrie' and there was a photo of her Australian friend with a short message: "What an incredible experience this has been! **Neither** I **nor** my fellow team members ever believed that we would work so hard, learn so much or make such good friends. Thanks, guys!"

2 Answer these questions.

1 What did Laura think of the website?
2 Who had it been designed by?
3 Had the university students produced the website all on their own?
4 What was special about the design of the website?
5 What did Carrie think about working on the project?

3 Remember!

Either … or / Neither … nor
Use these to express a choice between two items.

- Affirmative:

Either Ross or Laura will make the phone call.
Holly would like to learn either French or Spanish.

- Negative:

Neither Jack nor Holly came to the meeting.
The boys' behaviour is neither clever nor funny.

Make sentences using either … or …

1 You can look at the photo gallery or you can look at the message board.
You can look at either the photo gallery or the message board.
2 Holly will send a text or Jack will send a text.
3 You can write a letter or you can send an email.
4 The students can start their presentations or finish their homework.

4 Make sentences using neither … nor …

1 Carrie wasn't afraid of hard work and her fellow team members weren't either.
Neither Carrie nor her fellow team members were afraid of hard work.
2 Ross can't speak German and he can't speak Thai.
3 The film wasn't amusing and it wasn't interesting.
4 Jack didn't speak to Holly and he didn't speak to Laura.

5 Remember!

Past perfect passive
We use the past perfect for actions which happened before another action in the past.
I saw the tree which had been blown down by the wind.
The police arrived soon after the crime had been committed.
When we want to say who performed the action, we use *by* + noun.
I knew that the window had been broken by a burglar.

Use your own ideas to finish these sentences. Use the past perfect passive.

1 The police found the jewellery which …
The police found the jewellery which had been stolen from the house.
2 I met a man who …
3 We ate grilled fish which …
4 The new bridge collapsed soon after …
5 She refused to wear the dress until …
6 When he arrived at the house, he saw that …

Party!
Saturday 4 pm

1 🔊 2.22 Listen and read.

Laura: Have some fruit punch, Holly. It's **very** tasty.

Holly: Thanks. Mmm … It's **really** tasty. Did you make it yourself?

Laura: Yes, I did. With a bit of help from Mum.

Ross: Can I have some?

Laura: Of course. Here you are.

Ross: Mmm … It's **quite** nice.

Laura: Don't sound so surprised!

Jack: Is Professor Brown coming?

Ross: Yes, he'll be here soon. He phoned to say he's had a **rather** busy day so he'll be **a bit** late.

Holly: The website designers are coming, too.

Jack: Great! They've worked **incredibly** hard on the site.

Holly: Oh! That's my phone! It's Sergei! Hi Sergei! How are you? Sorry! I can't hear you **very** well. It's **pretty** noisy in here.

Jack: Hey, everyone! I've just had a text from Sofia. They're having a party in Rio, too! She says it's **extremely** hot there so they're celebrating on the beach.

Laura: How fantastic!

Ross: Three cheers for Global Youth Link!

2 Cover the text and say if these sentences are true or false. Check your answers. Correct the false statements.

1 According to Holly the fruit punch is not tasty. ___
2 Professor Brown is going to arrive very late. ___
3 The website designers won't be going to the party. ___
4 They have not worked very hard on the website. ___
5 Sofia phones from Rio. ___
6 The Brazilian team are celebrating on the beach. ___

3 Complete these sentences with words from the box.

> **too loud   terribly well   rather interesting**
> **so sad   extremely lazy   highly unlikely**
> **completely exhausted   incredibly fast**

1 He failed his exams because he is …
2 I thought the film would be boring. In fact it was …
3 He broke the world record by running …
4 Holly cried because the story was …
5 I enjoyed the performance but the music was …
6 She was nervous about the test but she did …
7 He said he would come to the party bit I think it's …
8 After crossing the desert on foot the travellers were …

4 Express your opinions by making sentences about the pictures. Use the given adjectives and an adverb of degree from the box. Compare your opinions with those of your friends.

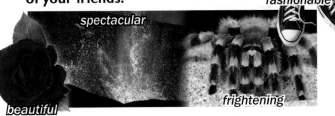

fashionable

spectacular

frightening

beautiful

not particularly   quite   pretty   really   incredibly

Remember!
Adverbs of degree

With adjectives:
*In summer the weather is **very** hot.*
*This book is **quite** interesting.*

With adverbs:
*He plays the guitar **fairly** well.*
*She speaks **rather** quietly.*

From weak to strong:
fairly → quite / rather → very → really → extremely

More adverbs of degree:
a bit / a little, pretty, so, incredibly, unbelievably, terribly, awfully, unusually, absolutely, surprisingly, particularly

▶ **Grammar extra p130**

Writing

Features of evaluative writing

> **At the beginning of this book you read about the website project. Students from all over the world met in New York and were given a task:**
>
> *'You're going to create a young people's website with a worldwide perspective.'*
>
> **You have now seen part of the website and your task is to** evaluate **it.**

▸ **What is evaluative writing?**

When you **evaluate** something you think carefully about it and make a judgement about its value, importance or quality.

▸ **How will you evaluate the website pages?**

- The first thing to think about is its **purpose**. What is the website supposed to do?

    a It is supposed to be based on four subject areas:

| ART | SCIENCE | ENVIRONMENT | EDUCATION |

    b It is supposed to present the students' 'thoughts and ideas' on these subject areas, the role in their lives now and in the future.

    c People should be able to 'access the material, respond to it and add to it.'

  Does the website do its job? Is it **fit for purpose**?

- The second thing to think about is the **audience**. Who is the website supposed to be aimed at?

    > When the website goes live, **young people around the world** will be able to access the material …

'Young people around the world' are the target audience. Will it attract the **target audience**?

- The **content** of the website is very important. You need to take each aspect of the content, describe it briefly and say what you think about it.

    a the project bar – How it started / New York, etc.
    b personal message
    c a message from the website creators
    d views

- While you evaluate the contents you can make **comments** where you think:

    a it is very successful.
    b it could be improved.

Where you think something is successful, explain your **reasons**.
Where you think something could be improved, give **suggestions**.

- As well as evaluating the contents, you should also look carefully at the **layout and illustrations**. Web pages should be attractive. The material should be clearly laid out and links to other subjects easy to find. Use of illustrations – photographs, charts, maps, drawing, etc. – should add to the information given.

- Your **final paragraph** should sum up your evaluation of the website.

    On the whole, I think the purpose of the website was very [clear / unclear]. It was [suitable / unsuitable] for the young audience. The content was [dull / interesting] and the layout was [attractive / confusing]. One area that could be improved are the links by using different [colours / fonts] to guide the reader.

Writing together

> You have looked carefully at some web pages from the **Global Youth Link** website and have read and discussed how to evaluate them. As a class, you are now going to produce a written evaluation of the web pages.

Things to think about. Make notes.

First paragraph: Write a brief description of what you are evaluating.

Purpose: Explain what the purpose is.
Make a judgement about whether it is successful.
- Are all the four areas included?
- Do the students relate them to their own lives?
- Have other people responded?

Audience: Explain who the audience is.
Do you think the intended audience will be interested in this website? Why? / Why not?

Content: Describe the different aspects of the content.
- Are they interesting and varied?
- Are they giving you new information?
- Do you think there is clear navigation? Can you easily find what you are looking for?

Comments: After a brief description of each aspect of the contents, say what you think.
- If you think something is successful, explain why.
- If you think something could be better, make some suggestions about how it could be improved.

Layout and illustrations: Is the layout attractive? Is it easy for the reader to use?
Is it too cluttered? Should there be less material on the pages?
Are the illustrations helpful? Are they too small? Do they take up too much space? Are there other illustrations you think would be helpful?

Final paragraph: Sum up your evaluation of the web pages. Include what you think is successful and areas where you think it could be improved.

Write your evaluation.

Remember!
- Make it clear **what you are evaluating** in your first paragraph.
- Keep the descriptions of the purpose, audience, content, etc. **brief**. The important part of the evaluation is **what you think**.
- Use your **final paragraph** to **sum up** how you have evaluated the web pages.

WB p119

Conversation practice

1 **Ross and Laura are talking. Look at the pictures and the words in the box. What do you think they are talking about?**

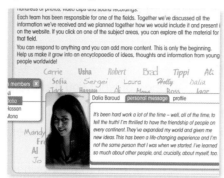

home page   colours   graphics   eye-catching
navigate   background   site   personal   click   leave a comment

2 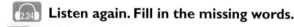 **Listen to Ross and Laura. Were you right?**

3 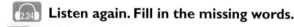 **Read the phrases in the box. Listen again and spot the phrases.**

couldn't be better   That's a plus   loads of stuff   don't you think?   Let me see   I'd say so   get involved

4 **Look at the Global Youth Link home page on pages 118–119. Talk about it in groups.**

Start like this: *What do you think of this home page? Do you like it?*

Listening comprehension

1  **Listen to some of the team leaders. They are talking via a video link about their favourite aspects of the website. Number these items from 1–5 in the order in which they are mentioned.**

science _____   video catalogue _____   education _____   New York _____   oil spill _____

2  **Listen again. Fill in the missing words.**

Usha

Ali

Robert

The _____ is absolutely _____! _____ to everybody!

Tippi, your film about _____ Thai dancing is amazing. The _____ are _____. I was _____ scared!

Carrie

Ali, I was laughing _____ at your feature on crazy _____.
Well done to whoever did the _____. They were _____.

The photos of _____ are really moving and the _____ with Brad's dad is excellent. It's _____ to hear from someone who was actually _____ and involved in the clear-up.

Brad

It's _____ interesting to find out how schools _____ around the world and it's good to _____ that some of us are more _____ than others where education is _____.

Individual speaking

You are going to talk about the Global Youth Link website.
What's your opinion of it?

Grammar extra

make or do?

Help!

Make up a sentence about the picture using *make*.

1 Complete the sentences using *make* or *do*.

1 Professor Brown is going to _____ an announcement.
2 We need to _____ more pronunciation practice.
3 It's too late to _____ any changes to your work.
4 Please _____ a copy of that photo for me.
5 The students must _____ a lot of research.

2 Write and say. Make your own sentences with *make* or *do* and these words.

changes   research   a copy   an announcement   practice

2

Let's look at come!

Look! It's from a dinosaur!

Make up a sentence about the picture using *come*.

1 What do the underlined verbs mean? Explain the sentences in your own words.

1 This extraordinary animal <u>comes from</u> Australia.
2 Deep in the jungle the explorers <u>came across</u> a hidden city.
3 The old book was so fragile that it <u>came apart</u> in my hands.
4 I can't meet you this afternoon. Something's <u>come up</u>.
5 How did your grandfather <u>come by</u> this ancient statue?

2 Write and say. Make your own sentences using:

| come from   come across   come apart
come up   come by |
| --- |

3

Let's look at set!

The kingdom will be mine – all mine!

Make up a sentence about the picture using *set*.

1 What do the underlined verbs mean? Explain the sentences in your own words.

1 Martine <u>set off</u> along the path in the direction of the waterhole.
2 The cold weather has <u>set in</u>. I must buy a new winter coat.
3 Thomas Jones <u>set up</u> his engineering factory in 1896.
4 As soon as they arrived in the village, the boys <u>set about</u> exploring the surrounding countryside.
5 An ambitious young man, James <u>set out</u> to become a millionaire by the age of forty-five.

2 Write and say. Make your own sentences using:

set off   set in   set up   set about   set out

4

Let's look at **hang**!

1 **What do the underlined verbs mean?**
Explain the sentences in your own words.

1 <u>Hang on</u> a minute! I need to do up my shoe.
2 Joe spent the afternoon <u>hanging around</u> with his friends in the park.
3 I was talking to my friend on the phone when she suddenly <u>hung up</u>.
4 You should <u>hang onto</u> these photos. They might be valuable one day.
5 The students gathered excitedly around their famous visitor but because she was shy, Lucy <u>hung back</u>.

2 **Write and say. Make your own sentences using:**

hang on   hang around   hang up   hang onto   hang back

Make up a sentence about the picture using *hang*.

5

Let's look at **take**!

1 **What do the underlined verbs mean?**
Explain the sentences in your own words.

1 In the washroom Kepler <u>took off</u> his jacket.
2 Sam is very good at sport. He <u>takes after</u> his father.
3 It's difficult to <u>take in</u> this scientific theory – it's so complicated.
4 Jenny has recently <u>taken up</u> horse riding.
5 Listen to the professor's speech and <u>take down</u> the important points.

2 **Write and say. Make your own sentences using:**

take off   take after   take in   take up   take down

Make up a sentence about the picture using *take*.

6

Let's look at **do**!

1 **What do the underlined verbs mean?**
Explain the sentences in your own words.

1 The wind was cold so Jane <u>did up</u> her coat.
2 The house is old and shabby but we plan to <u>do it up</u>.
3 We can't <u>do without</u> Laura as she's our computer expert.
4 I'm so hot and thirsty. I could <u>do with</u> a cold drink.
5 Sam's school <u>did away</u> with uniforms a long time ago.

2 **Write and say. Make your own sentences using:**

do up (1)   do up (2)   do without   could do with   do away with

Make up a sentence about the picture using *do*.

7

make or do?

It wasn't my fault!

I **Complete the sentences using *make* or *do*.**

1 Luke insisted that he _____ nothing wrong.
2 _____ sure that you don't forget your passport!
3 Harry is very disobedient. He never _____ as he is told.
4 Don't worry about the exam. Just _____ your best.
5 Laura _____ a very interesting point in her essay.

2 **Write and say. Make your own sentences with *make* or *do* and these words.**

> nothing / something / anything wrong   sure
> as one is told   one's best   a point

Make up a sentence about the picture using *do*.

8

*Let's look at **make**!*

We can't afford a car so …

I **What do the underlined verbs mean? Explain the sentences in your own words.**

1 Please, speak more clearly. I can't <u>make out</u> what you're saying.
2 Paul <u>made up</u> an excuse for forgetting his homework.
3 We haven't got any meat. We'll have to <u>make do with</u> eggs for dinner.
4 The thieves snatched the jewels and <u>made off</u> in a fast car.
5 Jenny bought some flowers to <u>make up for</u> arriving so late.

2 **Write and say. Make your own sentences using:**

> make out   make up   make do with   make off   make up for

Make up a sentence about the picture using *make*.

9

This marathon wasn't my idea …

*Let's look at **talk**!*

I **What do the underlined verbs mean? Explain the sentences in your own words.**

1 Professor Brown <u>talked round</u> Laura's parents.
2 She didn't need a new jacket but her sister <u>talked</u> her <u>into</u> buying one.
3 When an adult criticises you, it's impolite to <u>talk back</u>.
4 He always <u>talks down</u> to people who are less intelligent than him.
5 I'm not sure if we should go to New York. Can we <u>talk</u> it <u>over</u>?

2 **Write and say. Make your own sentences using:**

> talk round   talk into   talk back   talk down   talk over

Make up a sentence about the picture using *talk*.

10

Let's look at **pay!**

I **What do the underlined phrases mean?**
Explain the sentences in your own words.

1 This is important information so please <u>pay attention</u>.
2 Lucy looked beautiful but nobody <u>paid</u> her <u>a compliment</u>.
3 We haven't seen Aunt Jemima for ages. It's time we <u>paid</u> her <u>a visit</u>.
4 James <u>paid the price</u> for his laziness. He failed all his exams.
5 He <u>paid good money</u> for his new car but it broke down.

2 **Write and say. Make your own sentences using:**

> pay attention   pay a compliment   pay a visit
> pay the price   pay good money

What a beautiful smile.

Make up a sentence about the picture using *pay.*

II

Let's look at **hand!**

That's my diary!

I **What do the underlined verbs mean?**
Explain the sentences in your own words.

1 When Annie gave a presentation about her holiday, she <u>handed round</u> some souvenirs which she had bought.
2 Traditional recipes are <u>handed down</u> from one generation to the next.
3 When you have finished the test, <u>hand</u> it <u>in</u>.
4 John took the letter from Jane, read it quickly and <u>handed</u> it <u>back</u>.
5 The bank robber forced the clerk to <u>hand over</u> all the money.

2 **Write and say. Make up your own sentences using:**

> hand round   hand down   hand in   hand back   hand over

And very interesting it is, too!

Make up a sentence about the picture using *hand.*

12

say or **tell?**

Harry? Charles?

I **Complete the sentences with the correct form of *say* or *tell*.**

1 Can you _____ me the time, please?
2 It's wrong to _____ lies. You should always _____ the truth.
3 You must _____ goodbye to Aunt May before she leaves for Australia.
4 Can you _____ the difference between an American and a Canadian accent?
5 Freddie always _____ the funniest jokes.

2 **Write and say. Make your own sentences with *say* or *tell* and the**
following words.

> the difference   hello   the time   a joke   a lie

Make up a sentence about the
picture using *tell* **and one of the**
words in Activity 2.

Project 1: A portrait of New York

1 Use these old maps and the photographs to give you ideas for your portrait of New York.

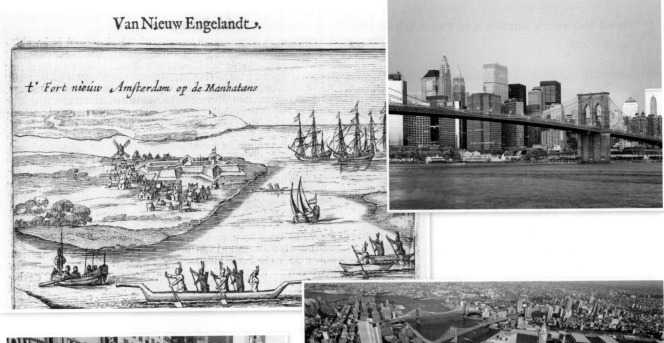

2 Find out information. Use these questions if you wish and add more of your own.

- How and when did the city begin?
- What does Manhattan mean?
- What is the present population of the city?
- What is 'Broadway'?
- What is in Central Park? What can you do there?
- You read a little about the Metropolitan Museum of Art. Find out about another museum in New York City.
- Use your information to create your portrait of New York.

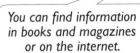

You can find information in books and magazines or on the internet.

3 Write your own views.

- What do you think is best about New York? Say why.
- What do you think is the worst thing about it? Say why.
- Is New York a city you would like to visit? Say why or why not.

Remember to start a new paragraph every time you write about a new subject.

4 Find or draw your own pictures to illustrate your project.

Think about sub-headings. You can use them to make your information clearer.

Project 2: Story writing – A day in the game reserve

One day, Martine goes with her grandmother and Tendai, the Zulu guide, on a trek through her grandmother's game reserve where Martine has come to live.

I Read the story outline and think about the questions.

They cross the grassland. It is hot and the sun is strong.
What is Martine wearing? How does she feel?
What animals do they see? What do they look like?
What does Tendai say about them?

They enter the green forest. It is shady but still very hot. What can Martine hear? What does she see? How does she feel in the forest? Does anything unexpected happen? What?

- They reach a river. What is the water like? What does Tendai say about it?
- There are animal tracks beside the river. What animals made them? What does her grandmother say about them?
- Does anything happen before they get back to her grandmother's house? What?
- Is it something funny, strange, dangerous, frightening?
- How does Martine feel when she gets back? What does she remember best about the day?

Remember to start a new line each time a different person speaks.

Don't forget to use speech marks before and after the words someone says.

2 Make notes about the story. Write the complete story of the walk.

132 Project 2: Story writing – A day in the game reserve

For a long time, many people thought there was life on Mars and that Martians, people from the planet, would visit Earth one day. No one thinks that now but people are still fascinated by this other world in space, which in many ways, looks like parts of Earth.

Mars is also known as 'the red planet'.

Remotely controlled machines called **rovers** have landed on Mars.

This is an actual photo of the surface of Mars taken by a rover.

1 **Find out information about Mars. Use these ideas if you wish and add any of your own.**

- Is Mars like Earth? How is it different? What does it look like?
- What do the latest pictures of Mars show and how were they taken?
- How long would it take to get to Mars? Are people making plans to try to get there? Who? How would they travel?
- Could people live on Mars? What would they need to take with them?
- Find out about *The War of the Worlds* by H. G. Wells. How long ago was it written? What happens in it?

2 **Write your own views.**

- Is it a good idea to explore Mars by robotic machines? Why? Why not?
- Should people try to travel to Mars? Why? Why not?
- Do you find the idea of travelling in space interesting, a bit scary or just boring? Why?

3 **Find or draw your own pictures to illustrate your project.**

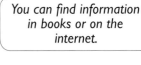

You can find information in books or on the internet.

Remember to start a new paragraph when you write about a new subject. Think about sub-headings. Use them if you think they improve your project.

Project 4: Play writing – A Desert Map

1 **The story of *A desert map* has a lot of dialogue. Luke's interviews with the security officers sound very like a play. Write them as the first scene of a playscript.**

- Remember, the playscript only has the words that are spoken by the characters. You can add stage directions to tell the actors how to say their lines or what to do when no one is speaking.
- Here are the first few lines to start you off.

Security officer: Did you pack this bag yourself?
Luke: [*nervously*] Yes.
Security officer: Did anyone give you anything to put in it?
Luke: [*stammering*] No …. I….I mean, yes.
Security officer: Which is it, yes or no?

2 **Write scene 2.**

- Use Luke's telephone conversation with Miranda from *Writing Together*.
- Write the conversation as the next play scene.

3 **Write the third scene.**

- Use your Workbook writing from Unit 7.
- Write Miranda's conversation with the man in the bookshop where she bought the map as a playscript.

4 **Write the next scene.**

- Some people come to the camp in the desert where Luke is staying with his father.
- Who are they? Are they the security officers who interviewed Luke or someone else?
- Are they friendly or not? What do they want? What happens?

Note your ideas. Write the scene.

5 **Read through your play with your friends. Practise reading it well. Perform it to the class.**

Project 5: The environment section of the website

In the environment section of the Global Youth Link website, Laura, Jack, Ross, Holly have included:

- rainforests
- coral reefs
- water use
- air pollution in cities
- an oil spill in Alaska

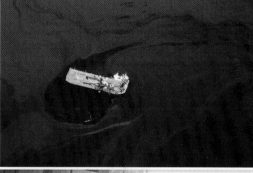

X Fix it!

I **Add your own information to their section.**

- You could add more about one of the areas they chose in the list above. You could choose something completely different to do with the environment.

2 **Write information in two parts.**

1 Write about one thing that you think is bad and that you want to see changed. Give detailed information about it so that readers understand the subject. Explain what changes you want to see and why.

2 Write about one good thing in the environment that you want to protect. Give detailed information about it and say why you want it to be protected.

Project 6: School website students' home page

Design the home page for the students' part of your school's website. If your school does not have one, imagine what it might be.

- In the Individual speaking task for Unit 11, you made choices about a website for school students. If you wish, you may use some or all of your ideas for the website to help you create a home page.
- Draw on paper or work on a computer to create the page. Write short notes to explain what information the different links or tabs on the page lead to.

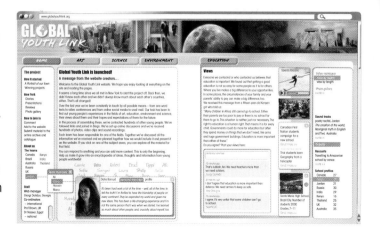

Macmillan Education
Between Towns Road, Oxford OX4 3PP
A division of Macmillan Publishers Limited

Companies and representatives throughout the world

ISBN 978-0-230-03253-8

Text © Mary Bowen, Liz Hocking, Wendy Wren 2012
Design and illustration © Macmillan Publishers Limited 2012

First published 2012

Concept design by Anna Stasinska
Page design, layout and art editing by Wild Apple Design Ltd.
Illustrated by Adrian Barclay (Beehive) pp78, 79, 127, 128, 129, 130. Martin
Bustamante (Advocate) pp5, 45. Grace Chen (Sylvie Poggio) pp11, 43, 71. Kay
Dixey (Graham Cameron) pp58, 59, 62, 64. Peter Dobbin (Pickled Ink) pp28,
29, 31, 32, 34, 42, 48, 49, 52t, 65, 68, 69, 72, 74, 108, 109, 112, 116, 134. Anna
Hancock (Beehive) p6, and character heads throughout. Kate Rochester (Pickled
Ink) pp15, 22, 38, 41, 95. Mark Ruffle pp8, 9, 212, 51, 52b, 121.

Cover design by Oliver Design Ltd
Cover photographs provided by Alamy/Rod MacLean(cl), Alamy/Perov
Stanislav(cr); Corbis/Stocktrek Images(tr); FLPA/MarK Newman(b & back cover);
Getty/Echo(tl).
Picture research by Victoria Townsley-Gaunt

The publishers would like to thank the Macmillan teams around the world and
Hala Fouad, Hoda Garraya, Caroline Toubia, Samira Maharneh, Adnan Bazbaz,
Nisreen Attiya, Mohammed Abu Wafa, Fatima Saleh, Muna Ghazi ,Anna
Solovyeva Yekaterinburg, Tatyana Olshevskaya Yekaterinburg, Irina Shikyants,
Irina Burdun, Elena Mitronova, Inna Daugavet, Olga Pavlenko, Svetlana
Potanina, Irina Ostrovskaya, Zhanna Suvorova, Sergey Kozlov, Olga Matsuk,
Elena Gordeeva, Marina Kuznetsova.

The authors and publishers would like to thank the following for permission to
reproduce their photographs:

Alamy/amana images inc p76(tr), Alamy/Robert Cole pp12(New York), 26(Empire
State), Alamy/David Cook/blueshiftstudios p86(br), Alamy/Victor Elias pp4(New
York), 26(tl), Alamy/graficart.net p135(cr), Alamy/Blend Images p5(bl), Alamy/
ClassicStock p57(tml), Alamy/imagebroker p86(bml), Alamy/Douglas Lander
pp98(br) 100, Alamy/i love images/gardening p27(tr), Alamy/MBI pp5(cm),
106(bm), Alamy/Rod McLean p89(cb), Alamy/Picture Partners p4(br), 22, Alamy/
RubberBall p56(tcr), Alamy/Alex Segre p26(cmr), Alamy/Travel Pictures p53(cr),
Alamy/Catchlight Visual Services pp5(cl),106(br),126(Brad), Alamy/Perov Stanislav
p66(cl), Alamy/V&A Images pp18(tr), Alamy/H. Mark Weidman Photography
p8(tml), Alamy/Gary Woodsc p46(cm), Alamy/Rob Walls p117(cl); Art Directors/
Helene Rogers p106(tr); BANANASTOCK p8(tmr); Brand X Pictures p86(bl),
135(cm); Corbis p67(tr), Corbis/John A. Angelillo pp17(br), 25(br), Corbis/
Pierre Colombel p115, Corbis/Peter Cook/VIEW p46(tl), Corbis/Ashley Cooper
p36(bl), Corbis/Jim Craigmyle pp7(tr),102(tl), Corbis/Julie Dermansky p106(tml),
Corbis/Neil Emmerson/Robert Harding World Imagery p38(bm), Corbis/Randy
Faris p86(tml, bm), Corbis/Natalie Fobes p135(tr), Corbis/the food passionates
p96(tl), Corbis/Edith Held p97(tm), Corbis/So Hing-Keung p39(tl), Corbis/Hufton
+ Crow/VIEW p46(tm), Corbis/Frans Lanting p132(tl), 132(c), Corbis/Jean-Pierre
Lescourret p39(br), Corbis/Tina Miguel/Nordicphotos p16(cr), Corbis/Museum of
the City of New York p131(tl), Corbis/Zhang Jun/Xinhua Press p117(tm), Corbis/
Ocean p107(tr), Corbis/Doug Pearson/JAI p17(tr), Corbis/Photolibrary p36(tcr,
tcl), Corbis/Radius Images p87(br), Corbis/Tomas Rodriguez p107(tm), Corbis/
Alan Schein Photography p20, Corbis/Image Source pp7(http), 86(bcm), Corbis/
Skyscan p88(tl), Corbis/Stocktrek Images p76(tml), Corbis/Luca I. Tettoni pp38(cr),
40, Corbis/David Jay Zimmerman p131(tl); CREATAS p86(tl); DigitalStock/
Corbis p36(tl); Digital Vision p133(tl); FLPA/Reinhard Dirscherl p135(tm), FLPA/
Mark Newman p106(tmr); Getty pp16(tl), 37(cr), 86(tmr), 119(tcm), Getty Images
pp37(tr), 96(cr), 98(tl), 99(br), 102(tr), Getty Images/Asia Images p66(tmr), Getty
Images/Michael Blann p56(tr), Getty Images/Heron Cabral Lopes Junior p4(bm),
Getty Images/Leslie Clements p132(b), Getty Images/Dreampictures p107(tl),
Getty Images/Echo pp46(cl), 16(tml), Getty Images/John Eder p56(tmr), Getty
Images/Flight Images LLP p88(bl), Getty Images/Mitchell Funk p131(bl), Getty
Images/Steve Gorton p53(br), Getty Images/Jan Greune p57(tr), Getty Images/
JGI/Jamie Grill p66(tl), Getty Images/Jetta Productions p107(cr), Getty Images/
Dave King p86(tcr), Getty Images/David Leahy p46(tr), Getty Images/Richard

Lewisohn p16(tr), Getty Images/Marcus Lyon p86(bcr), Getty Images/Anna
Nicholson P89 (cm), Getty Images/Panoramic Images p87(tl), Getty Images/
RubberBall Productions p16(cl), Getty Images/KEITA SAWAKI/a.collectionRF
p39(bcl), Getty Images/SSPL p133(b), Getty Images/Stocktrek Images pp47(tl),
119(tr, tm), Getty Images/STOCK4B p66(tr), Getty Images/Tetra Images p57(tl),
Getty Images/Richard Watson pp89(tm), 90, Getty Images/Kathrin Ziegler p36(tr);
GOODSHOOT p35(l); ImageSource pp26(br), 131(br); Macmillan pp73(screen),
96(tr), MACMILLAN AUSTRALIA Primary Library pp8(tl), 10, MACMILLAN NEW
ZEALAND p16(cmr), MACMILLAN MEXICO\Stuart Harrison p8(cm); Macmillan
Readers/Jupiter/Stock Images p57(tcr); PHOTOALTO p86(bcmr); Photodisc
pp38(tr), 44; Photolibrary pp18(bl), 25(bc), 27(br), 27(Padifield), 35(r), 36(bcr),
37(br), 39(tcl), 45, 46(cr), 47(tr), 55, 67(tl), 76(tl) 76(br), 79, 86(bcml,bcm), 97(tr),
106(tl,cl,cm), 119(cm), Photolibrary/Zero Creatives p8(tr), Photolibrary/Datacraft
Co Ltd p26(tr), Photolibrary/Sherrie Nickol pp5(tr),102(tl),126(Robert); Pixtal
p135(tl); Press Association Images/PA Wire/PA Wire p77(tl); Rex Features/
Kevin Foy p39(bl), Rex Features/Monkey Business Images pp46(bcr), 77(tm),
97(tl), 118(tr), Rex Feateus/Geraint Lewis p56(tl), Rex Features/Martin Lee
p86(tm), Rex Features/NOVASTOCK p35(m), Rex Features/Julian Makey p77(t),
Rex Features/Steve Meddle p19, Rex Features/Alastair Muir p56(tml, bcr), Rex
Features/OJO Images p8(br), Rex Features/Design Pics Inc p8(br), Rex Features/
Action Press p27(cm), Rex Features/Alex Segre p26(cmr), Rex Features/Image
Source p66(tml), Rex Features/Mike Walker p76(tmr); Science Photo Library/D.C
Stefen pp99(tr), 101, Science Photo Library/Martyn F Chillmaid p117(cr), Science
Photo Library/Robert Gendler p47(tm), Science Photo Library/NASA p133(tr),
Science Photo Library/Martin Shilds p117(tl); StockByte p107(cl); Superstock
pp56(br), 88(cr), 92, 119(tr), Superstock/Stock Connection p4(tl), SuperStock/
Corbis p86(tr), SuperStock/Richard Cummins p66(cr), SuperStock/fstop p67(tm),
SuperStock/National Geographic p37(t), SuperStock/Robert Harding Photolibrary
pp17(cr), 25(bl), SuperStock/Imagebroker.net pp17(cityscape),118(tl), 96(cm),
SuperStock/Image 100 p8(mobile), SuperStock/David Papazian/Purestock p119(b),
SuperStock/Pixal pp5(cr), 106(bmr), 126(Ali), SuperStock/Ingram Publishing
p86(bmr), SuperStock/Image Source pp5(tm), 16(tmr), 96(cl),106(bl),126(Usha),
SuperStock/Stockbroker p96(tm), SuperStock/Tetra Images p24, Superstock/
Trans-World Photos p16(cml), SuperStock/Travelshots p56(cr), SuperStock/Eye
Ubiquitous p87(tr); UBC Museum of Anthropology/Bill Reid p105.

Commissioned images by Lisa Payne pp4(c & bl), 5(tl,cm,cr), 12, 13, 16(tr,br), 23,
26(tr), 33, 36, 43, 46(tr), 53(tr), 56(tr,br), 63, 66(tr,br), 73, 83, 86(tr), 93, 96(tr,br), 103,
106(tr), 113, 116(tr), 122, 123, 126(tr).

The authors and publishers are grateful for permission to reprint the following
copyright material:

Page 115: Extract from 'Village Turns to Tourism to Save Cave Paintings' by David
Keys, copyright © David Keys 1993, first published in the Independent 14.10.93,
reprinted by permission of the author;

Pages 28-29: Material from The White Giraffe by Lauren St. John, copyright ©
Orion Publishing Group 2006, reprinted by permission of the publisher;

Pages 58-59: Material from 'Climbing the Mango Trees' by Madhur Jaffrey,
copyright © Madhur Jaffrey 1991. Reproduced by permission of the author c/o
Rogers, Coleridge & White Ltd., 20 Powis Mews, London W11 1JN;

Pages 48-49: Extract from 'Out of this World' Science Fiction Stories, chosen by
Edward Blishen, this selection copyright © Edward Blishen 1988 & 1991.

Printed and bound in Egypt
2016 2015 2014 2013 2012
10 9 8 7 6 5 4 3 2 1